Apollinaire

ROBERT COUFFIGNAL

Apollinaire

Translated by

Eda Mezer Levitine

Studies in the Humanities 11

Literature

The University of Alabama Press

University, Alabama

Translated into English from *Apollinaire,* Copyright © 1966
by Desclée De Brouwer
English translation and translator's addenda Copyright © 1975
by The University of Alabama Press
ISBN 0-8173-7322-5
Library of Congress Catalog Number: 74-2816

Contents

Translator's Foreword

This translation of Robert Couffignal's book has been for me a very profitable and enjoyable experience. An unexpected image of Apollinaire--not frequently echoed by his literary critics--is revealed through Couffignal's searching analysis of some of Apollinaire's works. Besides being a true exponent of surrealism, a first interpreter of modern art, an innovator of poetic techniques, a bitterly ironic critic of religion and religious matters, Apollinaire was also a poet who had kept in his soul a devotion to God, which, at times, he allowed to emerge with great poignancy.

As a final accent to the image of Apollinaire--the writer who relished research into the Cabala, the Zohar, the hierarchy of angels, and the exponents of primitive Christianity--it might be interesting to venture a possible explanation for the pseudonym, Apollinaire, chosen by the poet. True, it was one of his baptismal names as well as his grandfather's name. But isn't it also conceivable that the writer came to be fascinated by an earlier Apollinaire: Apollinaris the Younger, an author who, in my opinion, exemplified the type of personality that might have entranced our poet. Apollinaris the Younger was a fourth century bishop of Laodicea, in Syria, who, because of his ardent faith, became involved in an erudite and esoteric controversy with the early church--in particular, he denied the existence of a rational human soul in the human nature of Christ. What better literary com-

panion to Guillaume Apollinaire's Simon Magus, Simon the
Stylite, Enoch, Elijah, etc.!, and how appropriate to
choose Apollinaris the Younger as a namesake!

The translation of Apollinaire's texts presents many
difficult problems. The very essence of hermetic poetry
is to keep its secrets veiled, and isn't a translation
an attempt to reveal these very secrets? I have endeav-
oured to stay as close as possible to the French original in structure, choice of words, and meaning, but alas
--and inevitably--at the expense of the poetic element
which the reader, fortunately, can find in the accompany-
ing French version.

I should like, above all to express my gratitude to my
husband, Dr. George Levitine, Chairman of the Department
of Art at the University of Maryland, for all the help he
gave me in what appeared at times to be unsurmountable
obstacles in the translation. Without his insight and
assistance, these obstacles could not have been overcome.
I should also like to take this opportunity to express
my thanks to Sister Helen James John, Father John George
Lynch, and Rabbi Bernard Mehlman, all of Trinity College,
for their help in interpreting some specialized theological points.

Eda Mezer Levitine

Trinity College
Washington, D.C.

Chronology

"And you are also slowly going backwards
in your life" ("Et tu recules aussi
dans ta vie lentement")
Zone

August 26 In the city of Rome, a child is born who must
1880 at first bear a borrowed name, Dulcigni. A
month later, on September 29, after being
recognized at last by his mother, Angélique
de Kostrowitzky, the child is given the name
Guillaume Apollinaire Albert on the occasion
of his baptism in the church of San Vito. The
presumed father of the child seems to have
been, according to recent research, Francesco
(or François) Flugi d'Aspermont, whose elder
brother was abbot general of a Benedictine
congregation under the name Dom Romaric-
Maria.

1889 The young boy and his brother Albert, born
to in 1882, attend the Collège Saint-Charles in
Autumn Monaco, soon to be administered by the Mar-
1895 ianist Fathers. Their board is paid by Monseigneur Theuret, the first bishop of a diocese that had been under Dom Romaric-Maria's
jurisdiction from 1868 to 1871. Guillaume
has his first communion on May 8, 1892. In
1894 he becomes secretary of the congregation

viii

	and receives a first prize in religious instruction.
Autumn 1895	The Marianist Fathers, having participated in demonstrations against the president of the French Republic during his visit to Monaco, must close their school by order of Prince Albert. Many of their pupils enter the Collège Stanislas in Cannes, which is also administered by the Marianists. Guillaume (who is called Wilhelm) and Albert remain there until Christmas, 1896. Guillaume composes poems of religious inspiration including, probably, *The Death of Pan (Mort de Pan)*.
February to June 1897	Guillaume is in the rhetoric class at the lycée of Nice. He fails the *baccalauréat* orals. It is during this period, it would seem, that his religious faith is on the wane.
1897 to 1898	Much reading and writing of poems and stories, some of which show an antireligious feeling (e.g., *The Thief* [*Le Larron*] and *The Putrescent Magician* [*L'Enchanteur pourrissant*]). He embraces a Dreyfusite type of anarchism that rebels against traditions.
1899	Angélique, her sons, and a "friend" (Jules Weil) move to Paris and later vacation in Stavelot, Belgium.
1900	In Paris, Guillaume has difficulty earning his livelihood. As ghost writer for a serial writer, he composes several violently antireligious chapters for *What to Do?* (*Que faire?*). He claims to have written the story of *The Heresiarch (L'Hérésiarque)* at this time. He becomes friendly with Jews: Léon Cahun and Molina da Silva, who seems to have given him a few lessons in Hebrew. He boasts of sexual adventures.
1901 to August 1902	During a sojourn in Rhenania as tutor of the vicomtesse of Milhau's daughter, he falls in love with a young English governess, Annie Playden, and composes poems and stories, most of which will be collected in *The Heresiarch and Co.* (*L'Hérésiarque et Cie*). Bursting of the "modernist" crisis. Loisy's works (written in 1902) are placed on the Index in

1903. The Combes government (1902-1905) leads
the antireligious fight. Congregations are
expulsed from France.

1903
to
1904

A period of intense literary activity in
Paris.   He meets and becomes friends with
André Salmon, Alfred Jarry, Picasso, Max Jacob.   Suffers a sentimental crisis provoked
by the definitive departure of Annie, which
becomes the inspiration for *The Song of the
Poorly Loved (La Chanson du Mal-Aimé)*.   In
1903, Leo XIII is succeeded by Pius X, who
protests the law of separation between church
and state, voted in 1905, and condemns "modernism" in 1907, and later the movement of
the Sillon Catholique, to which Albert, Guillaume's brother, belongs.

1906
to 1907

During a period of relative sterility, A-
pollinaire composed two pornographic novels,
which are published sub rosa.

1908

He enters into a liaison with Marie Laurencin.   He publishes *The Putrescent Magician
(L'Enchanteur pourrissant)* and poems that show
a renewal of lyricism: *The Brasier (Le Brasier), The Betrothal (Les Fiançailles)*.

1909

From this year on, until his death, Apollinaire collaborates in the publication of
libertine texts among which, in the beginning, are those of De Sade and Aretino.   He
moves to Auteuil.

1910

He publishes *The Heresiarch and Co. (L'Hérésiarque et Cie)*, which receives some votes
for the Prix Goncourt. He praises the world
altitude record (1,000 meters) of the aviator
Blériot.

1911

He publishes *The Beastiary, or Cortege of
Orpheus (Le Bestiaire ou Cortège d'Orphée)*,
illustrated by Raoul Dufy.   Accused of receiving and concealing objects stolen from
the Louvre museum, he is placed in the prison
of the Santé for a week before being exonerated.   He throws himself into the cause of
modern painting generally and of cubism in
particular.   Pius X blesses the aviator,
Beaumont, who won the Paris-Rome race.

1912

With André Billy, he founds *Les Soirées de*

Paris. Marie Laurencin leaves him, precipitating a crisis that will last all summer. In April, Blaise Cendrars composes *Easter (Les Pâques).* Apollinaire prepares a collection of poems that he plans to title *Eau-de-vie.* In October, he reads *Zone* to some of his friends.

1913   Publication of *Alcools.* He is moving toward new forms of expression (simultaneous poems, conversation poems) and seems to have renounced his past. Charles Péguy publishes *Eve,* which is violently criticized in *Les Soirées de Paris.*

1914   He attends the performance of. Claudel's *Exchange (L'Echange)* at the Vieux-Colombier and does not appreciate this play very much. He composes his first calligrammatic poems. In August, the war breaks out. Apollinaire tries to volunteer. He is assigned to Nîmes, in the artillery. In the meantime, he has a brief but fiery affair with Louise de Coligny-Châtillon (Lou).

The *brigadier* Wilhelm de Kostrowitzky is at the front in Champagne. He writes numerous poems and a great number of letters to Lou and to Madeleine, a young girl whom he has met in January and who lives near Oran; he becomes engaged to her in August. In November, he becomes a second lieutenant in the infantry and leads the life of the trenches. He spends his Christmas furlough in the family of Madeleine, for whom, after this meeting, his passion will diminish.

1916   He receives his French naturalization. On March 17 he is wounded in the temple by a shrapnel and on May 9 he is trephined; a period of depression ensues. In October, *The Poet Assassinated (Le Poète assassiné),* a book written before the war and one that feels "alien" to him, is published.

1917   He is assigned to the censorship department and later to the colonial ministry. He is involved in the avant-garde poetry magazines. He finishes a novel, *The Clowns of Elvira (Les Clowns d'Elvire),* that will become *The*

Seated Woman (La Femme assise), and he pro-
duces *The Breasts of Tiresias (Les Mamelles
de Tirésias)*, a surrealistic drama--two works
dominated by his concern (sincere or feigned)
for the repopulation of France. He publishes
the poems of *Vitam impendere amori.*

1918   He publishes *Calligrams,Poems of Peace and
War 1913-1916 (Calligrammes, poèmes de la
paix et de la guerre 1913-1916)* and *The Wan-
derer of Two Banks (Le Flâneur des deux
rives)*. He finishes the verse drama *Color
of Time (Couleur du Temps)*. At the church
of St. Thomas Aquinas, he marries Jacqueline
Kolb, the "pretty red-head" ("la jolie
rousse"). He succumbs to the epidemic of
Spanish influenza and on November 9 dies in
Paris. His funeral is celebrated on the 13th
in St. Thomas Aquinas, his parish church. On
his tomb, in the cemetery of the Père La-
chaise, the following lines are engraved:

I have finally detached myself
From all natural things
I can die but not sin...

(Je me suis enfin détaché
De toutes choses naturelles
Je peux mourir mais non pécher...)

Apollinaire

Abbreviations

PW   *Poetic Works (Oeuvres poétiques,*Paris: Gallimard,
OP ᵒʳ Bibliothèque de la Pléïade, 1959).

PM   *The Putrescent Magician(L'Enchanteur pourrissant,*
       Paris: Gallimard, N.R.F., 1921).

HC   *The Heresiarch and Co. (L'Hérésiarque et Cie,with*
       an introduction and notes by Pascal Pia, Club fran-
       çais du Livre, 1954).

PA   *The Poet Assassinated (Le Poète assassiné,* with an
       introduction and notes by Michel Décaudin, Club du
       Meilleur livre, 1959).

SW   *The Seated Woman (La Femme assise,* Paris: Galli-
       mard, N.R.F., 1948: [This is a second edition,dif-
       ferent from the first one,which came out in 1920]).

QF   *What To Do? (Que faire?,* Paris: Nouvelles Edi-
       tions, 1950, with an introduction and notes by Ma-
       dame Noémi Onimus-Blumenkranz).

ANEC   *Anecdotes (Anecdotiques,* Paris: Gallimard,N.R.F.,
       1918).

TCS   *Tender Like a Souvenir (Tendre comme le souvenir,*
       Paris: Gallimard, N.R.F., 1951).

OC   Special note must be made of the publication of the
       first volumes of the complete works of Apollinaire
       *(Oeuvres complètes,*Michel Décaudin,André Balland,
       and Jacques Lecat, Paris, 1965). It is to this edi-
       tion that I am referring when I speak of Max-Pol
       Fouchet's Introduction.

Preface

In his preface to the complete works of Apollinaire, Max-Pol Fouchet seems to be expressing a current opinion when he says that religion had nothing to do with the elegiac of the *Mirabeau Bridge (Le Pont Mirabeau)*, the truculent storyteller of *The Poet Assassinated*, the experienced introducer of *The Masters of Love (Les Maîtres de l'amour)*. He writes: "Baudelaire torn by the double postulation of heaven and hell, Rimbaud inscribing his anathema on the walls of Charleville, Mallarmé denouncing the 'old plumage' of divinity do not succeed in freeing themselves [from God]; their violence, their revolt are still signs of attachment. How much more untouched Apollinaire seems to be!"

Is this really so? Is not the poet of *The Thief (Le Larron)*, the teller of The Heresiarch and Co. *(L'Hérésiarque et Cie)*, like Rimbaud and Baudelaire, in revolt against God and thus attached to this God? It might be worthwhile at least to find out how he freed himself from God. It might be worthwhile to define (as much as it is possible to do with a poet, and a poet of very diverse faces) the place of religion in his work. What is the nature, for instance, of Apollinaire's Christ? Something different, certainly, from the (almost) song writer's image seen by Max-Pol Fouchet, who is insensitive to Apollinaire's obsession with the idea of a Savior (as evidenced in *Zone*). In a period that encompasses Claudel, Péguy, and Max Jacob, it is a bit hasty to define Apol-

3

linaire as the least mystical of poets, and to affirm
that he cannot be placed in the religious universe of
original sin.

I do not claim to completely reverse the traditional
view of Apollinaire, in which he is seen as having been
dominated by a constant and conscious sensual joy for
life.[1] Nor do I want to ascribe to him any type of religious persuasion. But, after all, he himself exclaimed
one day: "I am a Christian, in God's name!" ("Je suis
chrétien, nom de Dieu!"). He was a Christian by origin,
by education. No prayers are to be found in his intimate
journals, as in those of Hugo; no discussions about the
subject, which his friends would remember. It is through
his work that we discover a pious child, a young man bent
on killing the God of his youth, a man in whom, during
the trials of maturity, this God—Jesus Christ—will resuscitate before disappearing for ever.

This misunderstood side of the poet's religion[2] has been
put back into focus by many critics during the last few
years—first by Marie-Jeanne Durry, who devoted several
of her courses in the Sorbonne to Apollinaire's religion,
and then by Michel Décaudin, Jean Roudaut, S.I. Lockerbie, André Fonteyne, and many others.[3] I am indebted to
these predecessors, and I should like simply to invite
the reader to a re-reading of Apollinaire's work, guided by the Ariadne-like thread that the religious theme
represents, being careful to note—from *The Putrescent
Magician (L'Enchanteur pourrissant)* to *Zone*—the leaps
and bounds of a dying God—a secret drama that brings
more sharpness to some of the stories of *The Heresiarch
and Co.* and more depth and pathos to the great poems of
Alcools.

1

Pious Youth

"What can one do to be happy
Like an innocent little child..."
The Song of the Poorly Loved

("Comment faire pour être heureux
Comme un petit enfant candide..."
La Chanson du Mal-Aimé)

"You are still nothing but a little child...You are very
pious"("Tu n'es encore qu'un petit enfant...Tu es trés
pieux"). these words from *Zone* perfectly summarize the
first years of the poet of *Alcools*. From his birth to
his seventeenth year, religion enveloped him in a warm
and cozy atmosphere, oppressive and yet sweet to the memory. Everything seemed to prepare the child who would
later adopt the pseudonym Guillaume Apollinaire to encounter the Christian God on his path--to the extent that
it can be acknowledged that a religion may be a help rather than an obstacle to true faith.
  "O Rome where I was born" ("O Rome où je suis né") exclaimed Guillaume Apollinaire some thirty years after the
day in August, 1880, when he was given life by a mother
who, for a period of time, chose to remain anonymous before recognizing him as her son. As for the father, there
is no mention of him at all. As related by the narrator
of *The Putrescent Magician:* "About the father nothing

5

was known, and she would not speak" ("Du père on ne savait
rien et elle ne voulait pas le dire"). Rome, a city
famous among all others, the cradle of Catholicism, a
privileged site and the justifiable pride of its inhabitants, was also the inhospitable land where no one waited for this child. Thirty years later, his Roman birth
will provoke a complaint that he confided to the rough
draft of *Zone*: "I have been feeling abandoned on this
earth since my youngest age"("Je me sens abandonné sur
terre depuis mon plus jeune âge").

Yet the newly born child can answer with a smile the
smiles of a loving mother who bends over his cradle. The
mother, Angélique de Kostrowitzky, after seeming at first
to ignore the child she had brought into the world se-
cretly, had him baptized on September 29, in the church
of San Vito, in the parish of the Basilica of Santa Maria
Maggiore, and had him legitimized on the following November. One can reasonably suppose that these actions were
caused by the pressure of religious scruples and that she
never regretted her gesture. During the early youth of
Wilhelm and of his brother Albert, born two years later,
she will endeavor to transmit to her sons the faith that
she had herself received from her parents.

The latter were Catholic Poles who had, throughout their
lives, struggled against the Russian invader--the for-
eigner, the heretic. It was in Rome, the capital of the
pontifical state, that they had taken refuge in 1866,
after the failure of the Polish insurrection. It was in
this city that, on the recommendation of Pope Pius IX,
they had succeeded in enrolling their daughter Angelica,
then eight years old, in the aristocratic boarding school
of the Dames du Sacré-Coeur, an order of French origin,
at Santa Trinita dei Monti.

Angelica spent all of her childhood there and did not
leave until the age of sixteen, when she was expelled because of her undisciplined behavior. One of her son's
tales, *The Blue Eye (L'Oeil bleu)*, alludes to these years.
In this story, an old lady describes the time she spent
in a religious boarding school, from the age of eight to
nineteen, and recreates the stifling atmosphere, the days
filled with prayers and devotional exercises. One can
readily understand how the young girl, when she came out
from this prenovitiate, intoxicated with her new freedom,

could have thrown herself into the arms of a sprightly
quadragenarian, the count Francesco Flugi d'Aspermont, a
retired officer. But one can equally understand how Angelica, having been marked very early by the stamp of
piety, could have preserved, throughout her worst trans-
gressions, some of her earlier habits and even some of
her earlier convictions.

They had first been inculcated into her by her family. Her father, a retired captian of the Russian army,
is mentioned in 1869, under the name Apollinaire Kos-
trowitsky, at the end of the list of the *camerieri d'o
nore di spada e cappa* of the reigning pope. He continued
to be listed until 1877, which must have been the date
of his death, an event perhaps precipitated by his sorrow at the scandalous conduct of his daughter. One can
readily imagine this faithful servant of Pius IX in the
role of Claudel's hero of *The Humiliated Father (Le Père
humilié*), Orian de Homodarmes, a refugee Pole living in
Rome. A knight in the old tradition, a defender of a
man under a suspended death sentence, of "an idol that
you call the pope" (une idole que vous appelez le Pape"),
he seems to have concentrated all his energy in the vi-
brant cry "Long live the pope-king!" ("Evviva il Papa
Re!"). Such must have been Apollinaire's grandfather,
such must have been the feelings of the Kostrowitzky family, the echoes of which must have rung, somewhat later,
in the ears of the child poet. A family in which everything gravitates around the pope, in which everything is
ruled by religion, a Polish religion reinforced by the
Roman milieu, a religion of principles and traditions--
temporal rather than spiritual, earthly rather than spiritual, incarnated in one man: the pope, the adoration
of whom tends to surpass the devotion to Jesus himself.

Thus, Angelica inherits solid traditions--or rather,
strongly rooted prejudices--of which we have several éx-
amples in the poet's life. The latter spoke several times
of the period when he was "a little child," and it was
when he wanted to point out some observances that one
would hesitate to call religious and that rather belong
to the realm of superstition--the wearing of medals, for
instance. In the eyes of the poet who writes letters
during the war to Madeleine Pagès in order to charm her
and to make her accept the idea of marriage, such a prac-

tice seems to confer the diploma of a good Catholic: "I
have on me the medals that mommy gave me when I was a
child" ("J'ai sur moi les médailles que maman m'a données
étant enfant"), he writes after concluding that the religious ideas of his fiancée and his own were the same.
Medals representing the Virgin, probably, which one hesitates to recognize in the medals he describes to Lou
somewhat earlier, in a letter filled with a wholly pagan
type of love.

The second detail noted twice by the poet in *Prayer*
(Prière):

When I was a little child,
My mother dressed me only in blue and white
(Quand j'étais un petit enfant,
Ma mère ne m'habillait que de bleu et de blanc)

and especially in *Zone:*

Here is the young street and you are still nothing
                              but a little child
Your mother dresses you only in blue and white...
(Voilà la jeune rue et tu n'es encore qu'un
                              petit enfant
Ta mère ne t'habille que de bleu et de blanc...)

is still of an external character.

It was an ancient tradition in France as well as in
Poland or Italy--in the provinces of old Christianity--
to dress the children whom one wanted to place under the
protection of Mary in white and blue during their first
two years. This had been the case for Chateaubriand in
a traditionalist Brittany and for Verlaine in Lorraine,
a region no less steeped in rituals. Let us note that
to this childish practice clings a piety toward the Virgin that can justifiably be described as an emotional attachment. The old bewitcher tells us in his *Memoirs From*
Beyond the Grave (Mémoires d'outre-tombe),[1] that a can-
ticle to Notre-Dame du Bon Secours, the first thing he
learned as a child, came back to his memory when he saw
the coast of Brittany, and Verlaine confesses that he
wants to love no one "but his mother Mary" ("que sa mère
Marie"). Apollinaire acknowledges the same love:

O Holy Virgin
Do you love me still
As for me, I know well
That I shall love you
Until I die...[2]   (PW, p. 576)

The poem *Prayer*, whose beginning we have just quoted,
reveals another religious practice that the poet's mother
must have taught him very early: an Ave Maria recited
every night, the pledge of eternal salvation if one is
faithful to a quasi-magic rite whose efficacy is authen-
ticated by a little story:

...The sailor who was saved
Because he never forgot
To say each night his Ave
Resembled me resembled me...[3]

Apollinaire writes this naïve prayer after losing his
faith: "I no longer believe I no longer believe"("Je ne
crois plus je ne crois plus").   What, then, is the meaning of this declaration of love to the Virgin Mary?   And
the insistence of the last verse! A last vestige of old
beliefs?   A puff of emotion when recalling an innocent
and protected childhood?

This piousness is due to his mother.   The Virgin Mary
is for him a mother substitute, an ideal model for his
own mother (who did not deserve total allegiance), a love
without reservations.   Others have been able to find in
God the father whom they had missed in their childhood.
Apollinaire transfers onto Mary the filial love that he
could not bestow, as he would have liked to, on a falter-
ing mother. Angelica herself always encouraged this devotion; even in 1914, she wrote to her oldest son: "Pray
to the Holy Virgin that she may protect you, and I shall
tell Albert to pray for you" ("Prie la Sainte-Vierge pour
qu'elle te protège et je dirai à Albert de prier pour
toi").

Thus she had communicated to her children in their youth
this piety made up of rites, observances, sensitive élans,
and spectacular gestures. If Marcel-André Ruff was able--
and rightly so--to speak of Baudelaire's "Jansenist cradle," one can be allowed to imagine for little Wilhelm a

cradle cushioned with blue and white, garnished with medals and pious images, surrounded by little angels and naïve hymns.

Piousness in the Italian manner, one could almost say a Mediterranean piousness, so much the more visible as it seems superficial, not always in harmony with life, and bypassing life without guiding it. Angelica sins against the rules of Christian morality but preserves gestures of piety and insists on raising her children according to the strictest rules of religion (at least in her eyes). Was the story teller of *Giovanni Moroni* thinking of her when he stated: "My mother was leaning toward superstition" (Ma mère donnait dans la superstition")? It is not certain, and this tale more likely alludes to a woman who was perhaps his wet nurse for a time.

At any rate, Apollinaire's religion will often be superstitious, more sensitive to the magic of rites and the vibrations of emotions than to the richness of dogma and to the intimate strength that can be given by Roman Catholicism.

Let us return to the story *Giovanni Moroni*. It tells of experiences that touch upon religious education and go back at first to when the hero was three years old:

> I remember the feast of the Epiphany.... This feast of the Magi, during which I ate so many candies filled with orange rind, so many sweets flavored with anise, has left me with a delicious after taste.[4] (PA, p. 145)

Thus, the pleasures of taste are linked with the Christian holy days--the first example of this union, so dear to the author of *The Heresiarch,* between religion and the delights of good eating and, more generally, between religion and sensuality.

The following lines allow us to understand the poet's love for the pomp of the church, which he displays in *Zone:*

> When I was not playing games, I sometimes said Mass. A chair became the altar which I adorned with little candelabras, ciboriums, and osten-

sories made of lead.[5] (PA, p. 154)

However, let us not overstress these experiences, common to many little Christian children and which famil-
iarize them--perhaps too early--with a universe of rites
and sacred gestures. It is not God whom this type of religion first discovers, just as it is not necessarily God
who can be seen in all the signs profusely multiplied in
the center of the Holy City: solemn feasts, consecrated
personages: pope and cardinals, monsignori, priests and
monks of all colors. These cassocks, gowns, the marks
of the servants of God, often speak poorly of Him and can
become obstacles to the discovery of the Gospel. Rites
can stifle the spirit; clerics who are unfaithful to their
vocation can scandalize forever the soul of too sensitive
a child.

Let us come to the scene that the narrator of *Giovanni
Moroni* places in his sixth year. The woman whom he calls
his mother has her fortune told by a monk who is more or
less a sorcerer:

> The monk was a handsome young man who wore a crown
> of thick black hair; his gown was soiled with wine,
> grease, and stained with little spots of dry and
> set dirt...The operation lasted half an hour, taking
> all my mother's attention, while I was attracted
> only by the card-teller whose gown had opened and
> showed him naked underneath. He had the audacity,
> when all the cards had been drawn, to stand up
> thus, bestially lewd, and to refuse the 50 centimes
> that my mother was offering while pretending not
> to see anything.[6] (PA, p. 142)

The hero of the story mentions other similar encounters
between his mother and this vicious monk, as well as a
visit to the convent of the Capuchins for the extraction
of a tooth. The latter episode ends with a Voltairian
phrase:

> The religious blessed us, saying that the teeth
> he was pulling were the only salary he was asking
> for. Since then, I have thought that these teeth
> most probably and very rightly became revered
> relics.[7] (PA, p. 149)

This is the comment of an adult, while the evocation
of the card-teller, so precise in its most crude details,
is something that had been seen. It transcribes a shock
that must have deeply shaken a young child's faith in
such a corrupt religion. The indecent monk of *Giovanni
Moroni* is only the first of a number of debauched clergy-
men, so numerous in the collection of *The Heresiarch and
Co*.

If one agrees to recognize in Francesco Flugi d'Aspermont the father of Guillaume Apollinaire, one is led to
believe that another cassock, this time an immaculate
one, appeared sometime before the eyes of little Wilhelm,
that of his uncle, the oldest brother of Francesco, an
eminent friar of the order of the Benedictines, with the
name of Dom Romaric-Maria.

On his father's side, indeed, the poet's heredity was
rich in religious traditions. Francesco had three sisters, one of whom was the mother superior of the Benedictine Convent of Ascoli-Picena, and three brothers, the
oldest of whom seems to have intervened several times in
the affairs of the irregular couple. At first he tried
to separate Francesco from Angelica; later, he supported
his brother's children financially, or more accurately,
he watched over their religious education by having them
accepted as boarders in the Collège Saint-Charles[8] in
Monaco. Dom Romaric, who had entered orders late in life
--in 1863, in the Monastery of Subiaco--was quickly honored. When Pius IX separated Monaco from the diocese of
Nice and established it as an Abbey Nullius, he gave over
its jurisdiction for three years to the Reverend Father
Dom Romaric-Maria, who in this capacity took part in the
deliberations of the Vatican Council in 1870. The Benedictines of the Congregation of Monte Cassino (of the
"primitive" observance) elected him bursar in 1881, ab-
bot-in-chief in 1893. He was to keep this function until his death on July 3, 1904. Here then was an eminent
personage whom one could not possibly suspect of any weakness. One must give up the idea of finding him in the
works of Apollinaire, even in another hero of *The Heresiarch,* the Benedictine Benedetto Orfei, very elegant in
stature, as was, it would seem, the abbot of Subiaco, but
with the great difference from the latter in that he was
gluttonous, sensual, and suspect of heresy.

It was probably Dom Romaric who, in 1887, allowed Angelica to enter her children in the Collège de Monaco,
ruled by the Marianist Fathers, and who succeeded in getting the ecclesiastical authorities to pay the tuition
of Wilhelm and Albert. The bishop of Monaco, Monseigneur Theuret, knew his predecessor well and had placed
his signature next to Theuret's on the documents establishing the new diocese. Thanks to the bishop's discreet
but effective intervention, Angelica's children were able
to continue their studies in the Collège Saint-Charles,
and then in the Collège Stanislas in Cannes until February, 1897, which is the date of their registration in the
lycée of Nice.[9] Thus, the supposed uncle was able to
participate in the religious formation of Angelica's son,
at least in an indirect manner.

The future poet spent almost ten years in this religious school, ten years that marked him with as strong a
stamp as that which his mother had received at the Dames
du Sacré-Coeur--but not necessarily a religious one. It
is easy to reconstitute the life of a religious school
before 1914 from the innumerable *Lives* of directors and
professors written by their Marianist colleagues, or from
the *Souvenirs* of their former pupils, such as François
Mauriac. One lived there in an atmosphere of warm devotion rather than of virile faith, of sentimental and os-
tentatious piousness that enveloped all the hours of the
day and spread over all the days of the week, all the
months of the year, in a rhythm of liturgy and a quasi-
monastical set of rules. The day began with mass, classes started with a prayer to the Holy Spirit and ended
with an invocation to the Virgin, and every night before
going up to their dormitories the boarders went to pray
in the chapel. Solemn high masses were held every Sunday
as well as Vespers and evening services in honor of the
Host.

This piousness is expressed in gestures and is addressed
to those toward whom all chants, rites, prayers, and
practices are converging: Jesus and Mary. It is the God
of Catholicism and of Roman Catholicism that Wilhelm
meets in Monaco as well as in Rome, in the nineteenth-
century climate toward which today's Christians show--and
justly so--a great deal of severity. The Catholicism of
that period is a religion created for women and children,

and Claudel, as a young man, feels nothing but revulsion toward this "old superstition." It was still a Romantic type of religion--the very kind that had so charmed Emma Bovary--sentimental and almost sensual, reduced to pious practices, emotional élans toward personages whose sacred aspect was all but forgotten. The dogma had become insipid through childish beliefs; the ceremonies were striking the imagination without even revealing the spirit of the liturgy and came close to being dramatic productions, moving and playing upon the senses. One can understand how they might have attracted the adolescents of the time, as can be seen in one of the verses of *Zone*:

> You love nothing so much as the pomp
>   of the Church"
> (Vous n'aimez rien tant que les pompes
>   de l'Eglise.)

This line calls to mind the high masses of Saint-Charles, the chapel choir filled with officiants, the purple of the chasubles and of the cassocks of the celebrants, the dazzle of the objects of worship, the glitter of the candles, the clouds of incense, the fragrance of the flowers, the moans of the organ, the sirupy singsong of the canticles, the platitude of which was appalling: nothing but declarations of love to Mary or Jesus, such as the too famous "The sky has visited the earth, My Beloved reposes in me" ("Le ciel a visité la terre, Mon Bien-Aimé repose en moi"). Let us reread the canticles of Abbot Lalanne that were sung by Wilhelm and his friends and that celebrate the Virgin:

> I want to love her, love her all my life;
> Until death I shall be faithful to you...
> (Je veux l'aimer, l'aimer toute ma vie;
> Jusqu'à la mort je vous serai fidèle ...)

Let us be fair: psalms were also sung during Sunday Vespers at Saint-Charles. And it was their Gregorian melody that gave to the future poet a basic rhythm for a great many of the poems in *Alcools,* as is stated by Max Jacob: "He had retained from the Fathers of Monaco the singsong of Vespers. It is on this singsong rhythm that

most of his poems have been composed." According to the
musical notation made by some scholars, it seems to us
that this rhythm came above all from the first psalm of
Sunday Vespers, the *Dixit Dominus Domino Meo*... Paul
Claudel also owes his verse, so close to those of *The
Synagogue* or *Zone*,to the same psalms:

> It is in the singsong of Vespers that I have found
> the meaning of this prosody borrowed from the
> psalms, which so exasperates the followers of our
> beautiful alexandrin...[10]

To this let us add Apollinaire's confidence to Madeleine:
"In school,*Athalie* revealed lyricism to me" ("Au collège,*Athalie* m'a révélé le lyrisme"). Was Racine's play
studied in the fourth class? If so, then the chorus
in that play would have communicated to the young pupil
of thirteen some of the feeling of Hebraic poetry.

Two devotions seem to have constituted the essential
character of Apollinaire's religion at that time: that
of Mary and that of the Sacred Heart of Jesus.

Because of their name, the Marianist Fathers spread
this devotion to Mary by all possible means: to their
pupils they distributed medals of Mary, Help of Christians, and they organized pilgrimages to Notre Dame of
Chartres. Is it possible that Wilhelm himself partici-
pated in them? Was his trip financed by the bishop of
Monaco? One can doubt it. However, would not such a
pilgrimage explain the strange verse of *Zone*: "Surrounded by ardent flames Notre-Dame has looked at me at
Chartres" ("Entourée de flammes ferventes Notre-Dame m'a
regardé à Chartres")?

This madonna surrounded by burning candles is indeed
the madonna of Chartres, and if the poet did not visit
her during his childhood, perhaps he did later because
he remembered her. What is certain is that he was admitted at the age of eleven into the Congregation of Marie-
Immaculata, a pious group established by the Jesuits,
whose members had to recite supplementary prayers to
Mary, such as the Little Office of the Holy Virgin. Wilhelm became the secretary of the Monaco group and, as is
stated by Louis de Gonzague-Frick: "He was praying to
the Virgin with a burning devotion."

He probably prayed in the same manner to Jesus on the
Cross, with gaping wounds--the representation of Jesus
favored by the Catholic iconography of the late nineteenth
century. French Catholics, more than any others, appre-
ciated this type of devotion, which was born in their
midst and was concretized by the Basilica of the Sacré-
Coeur erected on the hill of Montmartre in 1875. The
Marianist Fathers had their pupils recite "novena after
novena at the Sacré-Coeur," as can be read in the *Life
of Father Schellhorn*. One can understand how, in this
atmosphere saturated with religiosity, a crisis of mysticism could have exploded, such as the one that can be
seen in *Zone*. The adolescent stayed up to pray "all night
in the school chapel" ("toute la nuit dans la chapelle
du collège"); the end of the poem invites us to think
that it was in front of the image of Jesus on the Cross.
Those were, undoubtedly, unforgettable hours, a true
Galahad's vigil, the peak of a sincere exaltation, however forced by the pressure of the milieu on the individual. At any rate, this was a meeting with God, more
precisely with Jesus, God Incarnate, the Savior, the Redeemer.

The ceremony of Apollinaire's first communion was undoubtedly another privileged moment of his very pious
childhood, but it was marred, according to Wilhelm's old
friends, by an incongruous incident: it seems that Angelica wore such strong perfume that the audience was
troubled by it and that she thus caused somewhat of a
scandal. Even if this little story is only legend, it
points to the fact that the little Wilhelm had to suffer,
during childhood years, from his mother's conduct, which
consequently must have thrown him even more forcefully
into the school's atmosphere of piety toward an ideal
Mother, the Celestial Mother.

The picture of this religious education would be in-
complete if we did not speak of the thoroughly intellec-
tual religious instruction that was methodically dis-
pensed by the teachers of Saint-Charles and Stanislas.
Wilhelm accumulated during these years some religious
notions that seem to have been rather consistent. In
the fifth class, he was studying the faith, the stories
of the Bible, and the discoveries of science; in the
fourth class,[11] the Decalogue. He received prizes in re-

ligious instruction several times, the second prize in
1891. But we can wager that the stories from the Bible
captivated the poet's imagination before all, just as
they had done for Victor Hugo. He must have leafed
through his little book of sacred history with pleasure
and contemplated at length the engraved vignettes, a type
of Epinal images[12] used to illustrate the principal Biblical episodes. God the Father was represented as an
old man with a white beard, the Holy Spirit as a dove.
One could see the ascension of the prophet Elijah and
that of Jesus, the expulsion of Adam and Eve from Paradise and the cherubs armed with swords, the crossing of
the Red Sea, Daniel in the lion's den. Whoever skims
through Guillaume Apollinaire's work can find these pic-
tures. They are indeed the most popular Biblical images,
but they were revealed to the poet very early. Perhaps
he had even already discovered them, earlier in childhood,
in Angelica de Kostrowitzky's own religious handbooks.

A final evidence of Wilhelm's pious adolescence is giv-
en to us by one of his first poems, *Death of Pan (Mort
de Pan)*, composed, it seems to us, at the Collège Stanislas of Cannes in the last months of the year 1896. Wilhelm's teacher must have read to his pupils the chapter
of the *Quart Livre* in which Rabelais related the famous
word of antiquity: "The Great Pan is dead." The brilliant student composed a sonnet on this theme, the de-
cline of pagan gods. A faithful disciple of the good
Fathers, the adolescent affirms the superiority of Christianity over the religions of antiquity and immolates the
old gods for the triumph of the new God whom he salutes
as the God of the New Testament and whose disconcerting
nature he underlines: apparent poverty and universal
domination. Here, then, is a completely orthodox work,
one in which no personal accent yet vibrates. However,
it is not like a first draft of *Zone*, the poem that will
sing the primacy of Christ over other gods and His sov-
ereign authority over the whole creation, the poem that
will exalt the bloody God of the Calvary as the Pantocreator, the king of the cosmos who carries the centuries
towards progress. "Pan the great Pan is dead," the young
school boy sang. Pan will die again--and this time Jesus
with him--in a stanza of *The Song of the Poorly Loved*:
"The Great Pan love Jesus Christ/Are really dead" ("*Le*

Grand Pan l'amour Jésus-Christ/ Sont bien morts"), but
this great Pan will resuscitate, somewhere on the front
of Champagne during the war, while the God of Bethlehem
will remain buried in forgetfulness.

Such was the religious education of Guillaume Apollinaire. It permeated all the powers of his being--body and
soul, imagination and sensitivity. It is not enough to
say that this childhood and this adolescence were spent
in a religious atmosphere; they were saturated by it.
What was that religion? At first, an ensemble of gestures, practices, feelings, and beliefs, a highly hier-
archical social institution whose leaders are all-power-
ful--Roman Catholicism: colorful, effusive, spectacular.
One can understand how the young Wilhelm, born of an unknown father, grew up comfortably in its cozy and wel-
coming bosom. But did this religion bring him faith? A
childish faith, certainly, as can be seen in *Prayer* and
Zone and in the poems written in the cell of the Santé:
"I have just found my faith again/As in the beautiful
days of my childhood" ("Je viens de retrouver la foi/
Comme aux beaux jours de mon enfance"). A childish faith,
such will indeed be Apollinaire's faith, in the rare
moments when he will feel nostalgic for it: the faith
of every youth, a faith bound to and confused with youth.
The Roman Catholic faith in Jesus and in Mary, considered as invisible but very close beings, beings with
whom one can converse in prayer but whose transcendental
nature is neglected. Piousness rather than faith, a piousness that is satisfied with élans of the heart but
does not seem to emerge in everyday life or to impose its
mark on it.

This Christian universe, marvelous and imposing, reveals some cracks, particularly the scandalous conduct
of some of its ministers. Thus, nothing seems to have
been resolved at the end of these "pious" years: the
young Wilhelm, more than any one else, had all the opportunity to meet God in his path, and, at his level of
childish sensitivity, he does seem to have met Him during a memorable evening in the chapel of Saint-Charles.
Was it only a mirage? Was there not a risk that this
religion would become a screen between God and Apollinaire, a facade? And the regret that he will later dis-
play: will it be for the frame or for the central nu-

cleus of this Roman Catholicism? Such an education could equally stimulate faith as well as a rejection of faith. "One was taken, the other one rejected" ("L'un fut pris, l'autre fut rejeté"): Albert de Kostrowitzky, raised in the same conditions as his brother, in the very same religious schools, will be a fervent Christian all his life. He will not be content with only the "pretty faith of his childhood ("la jolie foi de son enfance") but will become a member of the Catholic *Sillon,* a movement founded by Marc Sangnier in order to regroup particularly generous Christians, sure of their faith, who wanted to transform the structures of society according to the Gospel and with the help of Christ. The education given by Angelica and the Marianist Fathers had thus come to fruition in the case of Albert, who was going to indulge in an active religion, who was going to become the "sower," the disciple of the "Great Friend," Christ. In 1914, Guillaume's mother invites him to pray and announces that she will tell Albert to pray for the poet. The latter recognizes the strength of his brother's faith; in 1903, he writes to his friend James Onimus, who had just lost his mother: "Since he [Albert] has kept his faith, he tells me that he will pray" ("Comme il [Albert] est resté pieux, il me dit qu'il priera"). But Apollinaire himself can no longer pray: "As for me, I only know this. I embrace you fraternally in thought and am sorrowing with you" ("Pour moi, je ne sais que ceci. En pensée, je t'étreins fraternellement et pleure avec toi"). These are the words of a man who no longer believes in God.

2

The Death of God

"When carnal and sacrilegious Carnival comes back..."
                                    The Dome of Cologne

("Quand revient Carnaval charnel et sacrilège..."
                                    Le Dôme de Cologne)

In February, 1897, both brothers enter the lycée of Nice, and it is then that Wilhelm, according to the consecrated expression, loses his faith. That is to say that none of his preoccupations are concerned with the religion of his youth, unless it is on a legendary and folklorical plane, as his friend Ange Toussaint Luca tells us in his book of *Souvenirs*. As soon as he is far from his religious schools, the youth completely abandons this Christian world. The pomp of the church and the élans toward Mary and Jesus are forgotten. The structure had been built on sand, and the childish faith crumbled all at once.

The poet himself has defined very clearly the reasons for his loss: "In matters of religion, the first lesson for doubt, for boredom, in a young man, is sin" ("En matière de religion, la cause première du doute, de l'ennui, chez le jeune homme, est le pécheé")(Décaudin, *Dossiers d'Alcools*, p. 19). These revealing words are very close to those of Georges Bernanos's country priest:[1]

Lack of purity does not destroy this knowledge (of God), it eliminates the need (for God). One no

longer believes because one no longer wishes to believe.[2]

This "sin" does indeed seem to be that of lust, and,
in a general sense, the abandonment to the urge of a de-
manding sensuality. When the poet confides to his mother, in a line of a rough draft that will not be incor-
porated in the final version of his poem: "I have taken
my sin from you, O mother" ("Je t'ai pris mon péché, o
mère"), one can think that he is speaking of the sin of
the flesh, to which the passionate Angelica had succumbed.
Only rarely will lust be considered as a "sin" by Guillaume. Thus, one must note very carefully the few traits
with which the poet seems to condemn it. In *The Thief*
(Le Larron), Apollinaire suggests that carnal instincts
are opposed to the Christian faith, which does not make
room for voluptuousness and which, in comparison with the
delicious pleasures of the senses, presents nothing more
than a cold, moral, and dull universe.

This type of conception could have had its source in
Wilhelm's religious formation. Indeed, if Catholicism,
at the turn of the century, was exalting sensitivity and
imagination, it still remained steeped in Jansenism with
regard to its conception of the body, which was looked
upon with suspicion and scorn; the greatest sin, in ser-
mons and treatises on morals, was that of the flesh. We
know that no man was ever allowed into Angelica's boarding school; we can be sure that at Saint-Charles the other sex was viewed with a similar distrust and even a certain aversion. The writers of the late nineteenth century protest against this reprobation. For them also,
for all the men of that time, Christianism seems to be
boring. Such is the opinion, for example, of Paul Claudel, who hesitated to become a Christian, to enter the
church, even after his finding God during Christmas of
1886, because of the yoke that he thought he would have
to accept.

How exciting the atmosphere of the lycée of Nice and
the possibility of reading contemporary authors must
have seemed after the quiet insipidity of Saint-Charles
or of Stanislas at Cannes! Apollinaire leaves an empty
shell; breaking out from the cocoon, he unfolds all his
potential in the sun; he feels free and can be compared
to the heroes of Maurice Barrès's novel *The Uprooted*

(Les Déracinés)--he recognizes in it the case of his
friend Toussaint.

He has already penetrated the world of writers and
artists that will be his world during his lifetime, and
in this milieu he will not find the faith which seems a
worn out notion, completely useless in life. In the innumerable readings mentioned by Toussaint Luca, in the
literary essays of these years, religion appears only
occasionally and on the same plane as other profane,
mythical, or legendary subjects. The Bible is no longer anything more than this "wizard's book eaten by worms"
("grimoire rongé des vers"), which is mentioned in the
poem *Reading (Lecture)*, written in 1897. Religion is no
longer the point of reference, the incontestable authority of *Death of Pan*, but a pretext for dreaming, for evok-
ing Lilith--Adam's first wife, according to Talmudic traditions.

One of Apollinaire's tales reveals his attitude toward
religion during this period. Later included in the collection of *The Heresiarch and Co.*, it must date from 1898,
when Apollinaire had just been reading several issues of
La Revue Asiatique. In a study by Karppe, published in
this journal, he discovered documents on the Zohar dealing with the names of the angels, and he used them for
his tale. He was so impressed by this reading that he
spoke about it much later in a letter to Madeleine: "I
really like *Simon Magus*; the angels in it play a precise
role, so scientific and divine, for which they have been
created" ("J'aime bien *Simon mage*; les anges y jouent un
rôle précis, scientifique et divin pour quoi on les créa")
(TCS, p. 103).

The young man who indulges in mammoth reading, composes a story in a genre popular since Flaubert's *Hérodias*: the Biblical tale. He writes a story *in the manner of*..., a work that lies on the fringes of Holy Scrip-
ture, following, in its first part, the seventh chapter
of the *Acts of the Apostles*. Contrary to what André Fonteyne has written, there is in this story no irony, no
attack against the Christian religion; it is, rather, a
good academic piece of work, brilliant and cold like
Parnassian marble.[3] The very sober text of the *Acts of
the Apostles* is enlivened by a sustained style with Oriental rhythms. The storyteller opposes Jesus's disci-

ples to the sorcerer Simon and already shows what will become a great obsession in his work: his attraction for personages with magic powers--maguses and sorcerers. Jesus is here more a worker of miracles than a master of life; he is "the one whose disciples accomplished so many wonders" ("celui dont les disciples accomplissaient tant de prodiges"), just as he will be, in *Zone*, the "Christ who soars to the sky better than the aviators" ("Christ qui monte au ciel mieux que les aviateurs"). This miracle of the Ascension is already announced in the story *Simon Magus* by the flight of Simon, borrowed from apocryphal gospels.

Facing the magician, the apostle Peter is described very soberly, and he has been given a rather handsome part. Nor is there mockery in the enumeration of the parts of the body of God, for this is borrowed literally from the Zohar: "The Order which is the Mouth of God...Tathmahinta, which is the left Elbow of the Body of God, Adramat which is the majestic Toe of the right Foot of the Body of God" ("L'Ordre qui est la Bouche de Dieu...Tathmahinta, qui est le Coude gauche au Corps de Dieu, Adramat qui est un Doigt majestueux au Pied droit du Corps de Dieu"), etc. The poet is having fun not at the expense of religion but with the jingling of the Hebraic names, the bizarreness of these appellations, just as he does a little further along with the names of the angels: "Isda! Auhabiel! Auferenthel!"

Another theme familiar to Guillaume Apollinaire, that of twinning, appears in the second half of the story. We meet two Simons, two workers of miracles, one a disciple of Christ, the other of the devil. The latter Simon is an ambiguous personage, related to the sacred and even more to the satanic; one could see in him a sort of antichrist. The storyteller seems to be more interested in magic than in religion; or, rather, in the latter, he is attracted, above all, by the spectacular more than by the transformation of souls and of social institutions. In *Simon Magus*, finally, religion is no more than a beautiful mythology, as it was for the author of Hérodias.[4] It is not the object of attacks, neither direct nor underhanded. It is evoked with an emphatic and solemn gravity--therefore, a traditional one--but it bears no evidence of the intimate convictions of the author.

Such is not the case for Apollinaire's first great
prose work, *The Putrescent Magician*, which contains a
violent attack on the Christian religion. We can speak
of it now, for the idea of this work must have been born
very early in the young man's mind, probably during his
1899 sojourn at Stavelot, in Belgium. It was during
this year, according to Marcel Adéma, that Angelica revealed his origins to her son. At any rate, the story,
which expresses a bitterness toward this illegitimate
birth as well as toward the burden of an undesired chris-
tening, spews up the Christian world.

Indeed, *The Putrescent Magician* is a counterfeit Gospel, a sort of Gospel in reverse. In the center of the
work, an antichrist: Merlin, who lies in his tomb and
"decays"--and a character of the story opposes him to
Jesus who resuscitated. His birth was a funerary Noël,
since he was born of a virgin and a devil. Toward him
there approaches a procession of three false Magi, guided by a shadow rather than a star and bringing sulfur,
salt, and mercury instead of the traditional presents.
The antichrist endures the suffering of the Passion,
emits a bloody sweat, and speaks, in a sacrilegious parody, the very words of Christ: "I am sad unto death, and
if my body were alive, it would sweat a sweat of blood"
("Je suis triste jusqu' à la mort, et si mon corps était
vivant, il suerait une sueur de sang"). A crown, not of
thorns but of hawthorn, consecrates him with derision.
If he has gone to Jerusalem, it is "by other roads than
the road of the cross" ("par d'autres chemins que le
chemin de la croix")--the cross, which he calls "an instrument of infamy" ("un instrument d'infamie").

Thus Merlin is opposed to Christ in spite of Apollinaire's baptism and even in spite of the fact that he
was a Roman Catholic: "I have been to Rome by other
roads than all those which lead there" ("J'ai été à Rome
par d'autres chemins que tous ceux qui y mènent"). It
is a corrupt Christian, a renegade who attacks Christianism, which is present here by its very negation. Throughout the story, the characters utter bits of Biblical
verse, but only to ridicule or contradict them. These
characters themselves belong to the Bible or to the primitive church: patriarchs like Enoch, prophets like Elijah, kings like Solomon, heroines like Dalila, anchorite

saints like Simon the Stylite. They are all ridiculous, grotesque, lewd, or skeptical. Enoch doubts that the promised Savior has come; Elijah, represented as a hermaphrodite, is accused of carnal vice; Simon the Stylite is given by Apollinaire a fate similar to the one he is subjected to by Luis Buñuel in his recent film: his virginity, symbol of inhumanity, is mocked; Solomon parades with erudites of love and recites an obscene proverb for which one would search the Bible in vain. When earthly paradise is alluded to, it is by the snakes that used to swarm there. If the Stylite recalls the law of fecundity proclaimed by the God of Genesis: "God loves those who are united" ("Dieu aime ceux qui se réunissent"), it is to hear Tyolet reply: "There's the evil!" ("Voilà le mal!")

Just as the "false magic gods" ("faux dieux magiques") are triumphant, the traditional values are destroyed: no redemption for Angélique, the young virgin who is Marguerite's sister in *Faust*; the pure heroine, not Merlin, is damned after a black mass has been celebrated over her virginal body, amidst a Walpurgis night worthy of *Là-bas* ("Over there"). Thus, from Apollinaire's novel emerges an odor of sulfur, sadism, and black magic. The surrealists who liked the tale partly because of this demoniac aspect were not mistaken. *The Putrescent Magician* would have no meaning if one took away its antireligious atmosphere, and it is correct to see in Merlin an embodiment of Guillaume Apollinaire himself, attacking a baptism with which he is obsessed, haunted by the faith of his youth, which he tries to get rid of by ransacking it. One can well apply to him the words with which Jean-Paul Sartre characterized Jean Genêt: "He lost his faith but not religiosity; the world must remain sacred so that all actions may preserve a sacrilegious character" ("Il a perdu la foi, mais non la religiosité; il faut que le monde demeure sacré pour que les actes conservent tous un aspect de sacrilège")--and, it can be added, so that his words may retain a blasphemous effect. The Christian religion appears to the reader of *The Putrescent Magician* like a deconsecrated building given over to a sabbath of witches and demons; an odor of decay is escaping from it, and of rape, and of despair. Is it the picture of the young man's heart?

The loss of his faith was the death of God, and it was a
slow decay rather than a renunciation without much ado,
as the conversations at the lycée of Nice and the evidence of Toussaint Luca would have us believe. Other
poems, other prose writings will convey the same impression, such as these lines from a rough draft of *Spring
(Le Printemps)*: "The cadavers of my days.../Some are de-
caying in Italian churches" ("Les cadavres de mes jours
.../Certains pourrissent dans les églises italiennes").

Let us look at a few poems written during this period,
approximately between 1893 and 1903. One of the earliest
of them introduces the same Merlin and his son, who is
a poet and walks with "his head haloed with fire on the
way to Rome" ("le front nimbé de feu sur le chemin de
Rome") (PW, p. 89). Must we see in this character Apollinaire himself? Must we read an act of defiance in the
following affirmation: "He will walk alone"("Il marchera
tout seul")? The meaning is too obscure for us to be
able to determine anything more than the haunting of a
Roman--and therefore Christian--origin.

*The Elegy of the Traveller with Wounded Feet (L'Elégie
du voyageur aux pieds blessés)*, written perhaps at Stavelot, gives evidence of regret rather than of bitterness.
Of course, the theme of the poem is the death of the
gods, and first of all the pagan gods:

> You are trampling the gods under your steps
> Walk and kill the gods as they are born...
> (Tu foules les dieux sous tes pas
> Marche et tue les dieux quand ils naissent...)

When Christ appears under the crosses erected on the
roads, the poet does not deny him: "You are walking
greeting the crosses" ("Tu marches saluant les croix"),
but he observes that the gods are dead:

> The sarcastic gods everywhere are dying
> And the magicians grow restless
> The flowers fade the fairies cry...[5]

These tears will be found again in *The Song of the
Poorly Loved*.

Another salute--an ultimate one--to a calvary, in *Passion*, a poem dated 1901:

I worship a wooden Christ suffering on the road
Tied to the black cross a goat is grazing
The towns all around suffer the passion
Of Christ whose myth attracts my adoration...[6]
(PW, p. 532)

Thus, religion is a human invention, God a useless
thing who is dying like all man's creations. The last
two lines proclaim the death of God and the death of
Christ, without alluding to any hope for a resurrection:

With the dying great pagan sun dies
Alongside the distant towns the
                    indifferent Christ...
(Le grand soleil païen fait mourir en
                    mourant
Avec les bourgs lointains le Christ
                    indifférent...)

Other poems not only establish the death of Christ but
provoke it, call for it, accomplish it. Such is the
case in *The Hermit (L'Ermite)*, which depicts an anchorite
wrestling with the temptations of the flesh. It has been
demonstrated how much this character resembles Flaubert's
Saint Anthony, the Paphnuce of *Thaïs*,[7] a novel about
which Apollinaire writes the following words in an article of 1904: "This novel, which ends with the atro-
cious sneer of a damnable saint" ("Ce roman qui se ter-
mine sur le ricanement atroce d'un saint damnable"). The
failure of the hermit, overwhelmed by lust, and the boredom that he feels in his life of prayer are fairly consistent with the mental state of the poet who saw in sin
and in boredom the reason for doubt. He seems here to
recognize that purity is impossible, that holiness is an
imposture. Does he go even further and blaspheme against
Christ, as his hero seems to do when, feeling the pangs
of sensual passion, he identifies with Christ agonizing
in the garden of olives?

I have kept vigil thirty nights under the
                    pink laurels
Did you sweat blood Christ at Gethsamene
Answer crucified one Say no I deny it...?[8] (PW, p. 100)

Indecent parallels that the poet, an iconoclast like

Rimbaud, likes to make:

> And I have laughed at the old angel
>   who did not come
> With an indolent flight to give me
>   a beautiful chalice...
> (Et j'ai ri du vieil ange qui n'est point venu
> De vol très indolent me tendre un beau calice...)

The Thief, a poem more significative than *The Hermit*,
betrays a personal conflict under the mask of legends:
the conflict of a young man, baptized, who is bored in
the Christian universe and is attracted irresistibly to
the pagan world, the world of pleasures and voluptuousness. His imaginary hero is a Barbarian who has stealth-
ily entered into an Alexandrine kingdom during the last
period of paganism, on the shores of the oriental Mediterranean. He has stolen the "sweet fruit" of the or-
chards. Let us understand by this that he has experienced the tenderness of women and, more generally, that
he has tasted the savor of earthly nourishment. How boring, in contrast, does his Christianism appear to him!
A place of shadow and of mourning, gray, cold, sad, bare.
It is the triumph of death and sorrow, and the god that
he venerates is a crucified god, the one who holds "the
sad reed" and carries a "funereal burden." Thus he is
not happy to be a Christian, though he confesses that he
is one. Christianism is no longer sufficient for him.
He demands that freedom of the senses which alone, he
thinks, can bring him to flower. This thief is not the
disciple of the resuscitated Christ, whose joy could illuminate him, but a follower of a dolorous religion, subjected to a law of privation and abstention:

> See the vases are full of humid moral flowers
> Go away but bare since all belongs to us...
> Go and wander credulous and rusty with
>   your shadow...9 (PW, p. 91)

Later, in 1915, Apollinaire will affirm his agreement
with a philosophy of life that he will oppose to the too
moral Christianism. In this poem, he does not seem to
be fully liberated, unless one attributes to him the
blasphemy of the chorus (that, for instance, in connection with the Incarnation). Whatever the case may be,

the poem sheds light on what Apollinaire's childhood religion meant to him on the day when he came out from his milieu, well protected from the drafts of the world, in order to confront a life of high winds. Nothing in his original faith had prepared him to accept this world as his own under the gaze of God, as Claudel will do; nothing even to recognize in the Gospel a message of joy and flowering, as did André Gide—excessively. The Christian of *The Thief*—and probably Apollinaire himself—knew only a strict and rigid code of morals; it was natural that he could not love it. As Claudel used to say: "And certainly we love Jesus Christ, but nothing will make us love morality."

In this poem, *The Thief*, paganism and Christianism are opposed as life and death are opposed, and Apollinaire strains with all his being toward life. He will often say, "We must not think of death, we must live" ("Il ne faut point penser à la mort, il faut vivre"). To him, Christianism appeared too much like a religion of death, the religion of a crucified god. The fat, sensual boy, which Apollinaire was, could admire the tragedy in the drama of the Calvary or accept disquiet as a form of religious feeling less than anyone else could. He did not appreciate the paintings by Rouault that were to "decorate Abbot Tourmentin's study" ("destinés à orner le cabinet de travail de l'abbé Tourmentin") *(Chroniques d'art*, p.54). Let us understand by this that he thought of the abbot as of the "abbot who torments himself and torments us" ("l'abbé-qui-se-tourmente, et nous tourmente"). Nor will he appreciate, to any greater extent, the works of Claudel or Péguy, both of whom, according to the strange words of one of his female friends, Roch Grey, he would gladly call "birds of bad omen who see nothing but ugliness and decrepitude" ("oiseaux de mauvais augure, qui ne voient que la laideur et la décrépitude").[10] Only in *Zone*, and then for a brief instant, will the Cross of Christ radiate an eternal glory and will the Christ of the Ascension carry off the round of centuries toward joy and flowering, in a joyous movement.

The Thief still betrayed a tearing between the call of sensual voluptuousness and the belonging to the religion of crucified Jesus: "Your only sign is the sign of the cross" ("Tu n'as de signe que le signe de la croix").

Such were the last words of the poem, derisive but
painful. In other works only mocking and disrespect
can be felt, as in the *Dome of Cologne (Le Dôme de Cologne)*, dated 1901, with its provocative beginning:

> Your last architect O Dome became insane
> This clearly proves that God does not give a damn
> About those who are working for his greatest
>   glory...[11]   (PW, p. 538)

Besides, the poet would like religion to serve the modern world, to contribute to progress, and this is already
a theme similar to the first line of *Zone*:

> But be modern and let your deified priests
> Stretch telegraphic wires between your towers...
> (Mais sois moderne et que tes prêtres déifiques
> Tendent entre tes tours des fils télégraphiques...

And the Eiffel tower is a point of comparison with the
cathedral of Cologne:

> Dome marvel among the marvels of the world
> The Eiffel tower...
> (Dôme merveille entre les merveilles du monde
> La Tour Eiffel...)

But it is not a hymn that rises up in *Zone*. If the
monument is a "marvel," the interior is a theater of the
grotesque and a crude spectacle indeed. It harbors ridiculous superstitions, such as the cult of (false) saints:
"You are concealing the decay of the Magi" ("tu recèles
la pourriture des rois mages").

Always, this odor of decay that arises from corrupt
Christianism! And the "carnal and sacrilegious" Carnival
penetrates into the nave where, near a holy water basin,
"a white cuirassier pinches unashamedly/The buttocks of
a young lady from Cologne" ("un cuirassier blanc pince
sans vergogne Les fesses d'une demoiselle de Cologne"),
where an adulterous husband is confessing his sins, where
the well-known prostitute Marizibill is making a date
with her "fat lover," and where other very unsavory scenes
are taking place.

The last stanza of the poem accepts the death of God
as a fait accompli by proclaiming that "man has created
the gods" and yet ends, unexpectedly, with a prayer to

the Virgin Mary, the "statue with tender looks":

> I have told the mother of God You who are smiling
> Place flowering rose bushes by the roadside
> And the rose gatherers will say prayers
> When the roads in May will become rosaries...[12]

Affected and sentimentalized? Of course! However, Mary
at Chartres, just as in the cathedral of Cologne, will
lower her eyes towards the poet with the same smile:
"Surrounded by ardent flames Notre-Dame has looked at me
at Chartres" ("Entourée de flammes ferventes Notre-Dame
m'a regardé à Chartres").

Must one see, on the contrary, a statement of irrev-
erence toward Mary in another poem composed in the shadow of the Dome: *The Virgin with the Bean Flower at Cologne (La Vierge à la fleur de haricot à Cologne*? The
poet describes a famous painting,[13] plays on words with
regard to Mary's virginal conception: "And one con-
ceives that she conceived from the Paraclete" ("Et l'on
conçoit qu'elle ait conàu du Paraclet"). Then, little
by little, he associates the young woman from the painting with the painter's mistress and with his own mistress, Annie Playden, the blonde girl with blue eyes.
This short piece, essentially a love poem, expresses neither piousness nor mockery about religious matters. It
is, rather a first evidence of the fusion that Apollinaire creates between the woman he loves and Mary, the
ideal model of womanhood.

What, then, is the God whose death Apollinaire observes
or even calls for? Is it the Christian God, is it the
"Divinity" of the deists? What divine face appears in
the works of this period? A youthful poem is called *God*;
what is this "God"?

> I want to live inhuman, powerful and proud
> Since I was created in the image of God
> But as a god I am very submissive to fate
> Which leaves me a regret for ancient instincts
> And predicts in my race a just and certain god
> Look from the animal a man is born unto you
> And the god who will be in me has become
>   incarnated.[14]   (PW, p. 838)

The second line alludes to the famous words of Genesis
("Yahweh created man in his own image"). Thus it is the

Biblical God who is attacked, through a radical reversal
of the spirit of the sacred text. The spirit-God of Genesis, personal and generous, becomes here the tyrannical
God, the monstrous and dumb idol whom Feuerbach, and so
many others after him, denounced--and justly so. If such
was the face of God for the young man, one can do nothing
but approve his revolt. In spite of the Biblical reference, this kind of God was not the God of Christianism,
for whom one can feel a longing in the poem: "this just
and certain God" ("ce Dieu juste et certain"). No incarnation for Apollinaire in the traditional sense, but
rather a personal divinization close to what was desired
by Renan, when he spoke of the divinization of humanity.
The thought is confused, but the attack leaves no room
for doubt. It is taken up again several times in a similar form in other works of Apollinaire, as for instance
in the feuilleton *What to Do? (Que faire?)*, to which he
contributed in 1900, according to his biographers. Let
us agree that the chapters edited by Madame Noémi Onimus-
Blumenkranz are by Apollinaire. They allow us to understand what God he was then attacking and, even if they
do not have great literary value, they express a violent
resentment against his original Catholicism.

Apollinaire creates a character, a Dr. Cornelius Hans
Peters, and attributes to him the following words:

> God! God! There is no God! I shall snatch this
> impostor from his throne of clouds and everybody
> will trample this old joker whom caricaturists are
> forced to adorn with a white beard in order to make
> him respectable for us. God is man...[15]

This God is indeed Jahweh, the one whom little Wilhelm's
Sacred Scriptures pictured with a beard, the one present
in popular imagination, and referred to in *Waiting for
Godot*--the old and feared gentleman, the tyrant who ali-
enates man. But the God who became a man in order to
save man is also not respected in the novel *What to Do?*,
and His very words are turned into mockery:

> Humanity likes only puns. Christ has said: You
> are Peter and on this stone I shall construct my
> church. You are fishermen of fish, you will become
> fishermen of men. Jokers! And what a language![16]

And yet many puns and plays on words will burst out through Apollinaire's work, and he himself will indeed be able to be called a joker. But in the passage just quoted it is Christian religion that is attacked through a Voltairian criticism that stops at the literalness of the evangelical text and refuses to understand its spirit.

Dr. Cornelius is only a character from a feuilleton, and one should not attribute all his sayings to his creator, if the latter is indeed Apollinaire: "For an instant, the doctor showed the pride that caused the fall of the angel of evil" ("Le docteur un instant refléta l'orgueil qui causa la perte de l'ange du mal"). This time it is the narrator who is speaking. But we sense less conviction in this stereotyped judgment than we do in the preceding virulent attacks. At any rate, this militant atheism corresponds to the atheism appearing in other poems of 1900, and we should accept it, just as Apollinaire does. It will not be without eclipses in the poet's life and, like any atheism, it is necessary to define it, not in order to discover an aspiration toward faith hidden under the blasphemy but in order to search for the confused feelings, the personal accents, that singularize Guillaume Apollinaire's attitude towards God.

This period of militant atheism, which lasts from 1898 to about 1906, began with a violent movement of revolt that was very understandable in a young man whose exuberant vitality had been denied too long. In a line of *What to do?* the cry of a prisoner finally liberated bursts out. It is the cry of an anarchist refusing the yoke:

> One should throw down all religions, destroy the idols, temples, superstitions, chase the priests, judges, and policemen...
> (Il faudrait jeter bas toutes les religions, détruire les idoles, les temples et les superstitions, chasser prêtres, juges et gendarmes...)

The equivalence between religion and superstition, between priests and policemen, sheds a luminous light on what this rejection of Catholicism was for Apollinaire. But this first burst of independence is replaced by a

clinging bitterness, by a degradation knowingly and cold-
ly distilled throughout the stories written before 1906
and later collected in *The Heresiarch and Co.*
    One cannot explain this work only in terms of the in-
fluence of Marcel Schwob, Villiers de l'Isle-Adam, or
others. The subjects, genres, tone, and style of these
stories are very different, but the most striking char-
acteristic of the collection is the abundance of religious themes—or rather of antireligious themes. If one
does not count the polyptic types of stories, one can
find twelve stories out of sixteen that deal with religion, and by counting each individual tale, fifteen out
of twenty-three. Only two stories escape this obsession—two purely romantic tales: *The Disappearance of
Honoré Subrac (La disparition d'Honoré Subrac)* and *The
Sailor from Amsterdam (Le Matelot d'Amsterdam),* and the
most poetic *Que vlo ve*, a tale wholly inspired by the
region of the Ardennes.
    André Fonteyne, in his solid study, was able to speak
of the theological unity of *The Heresiarch and Co.* In
the very first pages there arises an avatar of the antichrist: Isaac Laquedem, the wandering Jew, cursed by
Christ and defying Him; and, in the final pages, a false
messiah, Al-David, a worker of miracles as powerful as
Christ, fools the crowds of believers. On every page
characters appear who are associated with religion,ques-
tions of theology or morality are debated, and scriptural
passages are quoted from the Old and New Testaments,
from canonical and apocryphal books, from Talmudic or
patristic commentaries, and from the Catholic liturgy.
In short, all of "religion," with its sacred books, its
ministers, its dogmas, its rites—but a burlesqued religion. Unfaithful Jews, heretical priests, derisory
beliefs, a stupid Bible: the negative is everywhere,
according to the title of the collection, that is, not
only in a heresiarch, but in all his company, which suggests a corrupt religion, a religion in reverse.
    Why is there any mention of Jews, if not for the fact
that Jews were considered, since the trial of Jesus, as
heretics, that is to say adversaries, or, if they converted, false witnesses to Christ? Indeed, Apollinaire
well appreciates the picturesque character and the out-
law condition of the Jews. He took the side of Dreyfus,

witness of a persecuted race, because he often felt close
to these uprooted people. Therefore, he loved them:
"They are pleasantly agitated and some of them are unhappy" ("Ils s'agitent agréablement et il en est de malheureux"). He often takes their side against Christians,
whose cruel anti-Semitism he stigmatizes. Thus, in the
story of *The Passer-by from Prague (Le Passant de Prague)*,
he describes the torture of a Jew who is about to be
hanged in Munich in 1334:

> The Jew had his head emprisoned in an iron mask
> painted in red. The mask imitated a diabolical
> figure whose ears, in truth, had the shape of the
> ears of a donkey, such as the ones which are placed
> on naughty children....No woman felt any pity to-
> ward the Jew. It occurred to none of them to wipe
> his face sweating under the mask--like that unknown
> woman, called Saint Veronica, who wiped the face
> of Jesus with cloth. After noticing that a knave
> from the procession was holding two big dogs in
> leash, the crowd demanded that they be hanged next
> to the Jew. I thought that it was a double sacri-
> lege, from the point of view of these people who
> made the Jew into a sort of heartrending Christ and
> from the human point of view, for I detest animals,
> Sir, and I cannot bear it when they are treated
> like men...[17]

According to the narrator, who pities the unhappy Jew,
these Christians are committing a sacrilege. As a champion of humanity, he can justifiably denounce the manifest contradiction between the beliefs and the conduct
of "those people." The narrator here is Isaac Laquedem,
but, obviously, Apollinaire takes his side, the side of
the persecuted Jews, against their executioners. He
seems to be fascinated by the personality of the wandering Jew. Here is a type of being dear to the poet of
Zone: he defies time, leads a quasi-divine existence,
never knows sadness. The narrator disapproves of Laquedem's excesses, of course, but he reports them with complacency, with a touch of envy for his zest for life and
his amorous exploits. Diabolical, the wandering Jew
glorifies in his genial sin: "Remorse? What for? Keep
the peace of your soul and be evil. The good will thank

you for it. Christ! I have flouted him. He made me
superhuman" ("Des remords? Pourquoi? Gardez la paix de
l'âme et soyez méchant. Les bons vous en sauront gré.
Le Christ! Je l'ai bafoué. Il m'a fait surhumain").
Here then is a perfect type of immoralist. Let us un-
derline the fact that he is so *against* Christ.

Another immoralist, the Latin Jew in the story by that
name, is a bad Jew--a renegade--and a bad Christian,
since he is a dangerous criminal. If the wandering Jew
poses as a Don Quixote of immoralism, Gabriel Fernisoun
has the rotundity of Sancho Panza. Sensual above all, a
joyful gourmand, he rejects the prescriptions of the
Leviticus, knows nothing of the Jewish religion, confesses to a liking for the Christian religion because of
its wonders: "The story of the Sacred Heart causes my
ancient Latin Jewish soul, in love with theophanies and
anthropomorphisms, to be delirious"("L'histoire du Sacré-
Coeur fait délirer mon âme ancienne de juif latin, épris
des théophanies et des anthropomorphismes"). But his profession of immoralism is even more worrisome than that
of Isaac Laquedem, who exhibited some sort of grandeur
in his debauchery. Here there is lowness and cowardice,
a quasi-superstitious belief in the automatic efficacity
of the sacraments:

> I no longer hope for the Messiah, but I hope for
> Baptism. This hope gives me all possible joys. I
> live fully. I amuse myself superbly. I thieve,
> I kill, I rip women open, I violate sepulchers,but
> I shall go to Paradise,for I am hoping for Baptism,
> and the Kaddish will not be said at my death...[18]

Another Jew who degrades religion, his own first of
all, and the religion of Christians, by considering it as
an insurance for eternal life and at the same time as a
reservoir of magic apparitions.

Finally, if Al-David, the hero of *To Touch at a Distance (Toucher à distance)*, is not a Jew but a baron of
Ormesan, his story highlights the Jewish point of view
at the expense of the Christian: "A certain number of
Jewish communities from the five parts of the world took
(him) for the Messiah." ("Un certain nombre de commu-
nautés juives des cinq parties du Monde [le] prirent pour
le Messie.") This prophet fulfills the hope of the Jews,

but it is calculated to deceive them, for he reveals himself as a false prophet. To avenge the Jews for this betrayal, the narrator kills the pseudoprophet with gunshots; thus dies a true messiah--but is it the true one or the false? Does not the shot hit the true messiah under the appearance of the false one? At any rate, the Christians are ridiculed in this tale whose climax is a sort of match between Al-David and a monk who vainly attempts to exorcise him. The pope himself loses face by not breathing a word of the affair--which, however, has been divulged to the entire world.

Thus the Jews seem to incarnate some of Apollinaire's ideas. He never unites with them, but he uses them as mouthpieces, reminiscent of those Voltairian puppets who cannot themselves be taken seriously but whose reactions often translate the reactions of the storyteller.

Such is also the case for the ecclesiastics of all ranks and cloth who circulate through the stories of *The Heresiarch and Co.* It is against them, without any possible doubt, that the author's anticlerical verve is relentlessly directed, contrary to his attitude towards the Jews. Sensual and skeptical high prelates, superstitious priests, concupiscent monks--what a gallery of cheats and vicious people, what a scandalous church! If the church is really such, one is grateful to the author for denouncing its faults and cleaning out its stains! But Apollinaire is not a Bernanos. He does not hope for the church to reform, he notes its decay with a sort of violent joy, in the manner of a Luis Buñuel. These mitered abbots of *The Golden Age,* mumbling prayers through the bones of their skeletons, remnants of a moribund universe, were already those of the stories of *The Heresiarch and Co.*

Honor to whom honor is due: the pope of *Infallibility* (*L'Infaillibilité*), the custodian of a formidable power founded on ruse, is an unadulterated politician, a sly Italian who keeps silent in order to hide his game and dissimulate his feelings; an inflexible keeper of congealed dogmas, he excommunicates heretics, but well knows how to coax rebels by showering them with honors. A pope based more on imagination than observation, for one would have difficulty in recognizing in him Pope Pius X, who had been reigning since 1903. The latter would be closer

to the pope who is described in the story of *The Poet
Assassinated:* a kind old man, "white head of the old
church, snow that Catholics think to be eternal, a hot-
house lily"("tête blanche de la vieille Eglise,neige que
les catholiques pensent éternelle, lys en serre"). Here,
the tone is emphatic rather than critical--a bit mocking.
So much the more surprising will be the dithyrambic salute
to "the most modern European, Pope Pius X" that we hear
in the first lines of *Zone.*

The high dignitaries of the Catholic church--cardinals,
bishops, the various prelates--possess more riches and
power than true faith. The archbishop of Paris, according to the narrator of *The Latin Jew (Le Juif latin),*"has
just inherited Fernisoun's very large fortune" ("vient
d'hériter la très grosse fortune de Fernisoun"), and
can only encourage the converted Jew's request for canonization. Cardinal Porporelli, in *Infallibility,* wishes only for tranquility. He hardly understands the torments of the reformers of Christianity and snoozes, after a good meal, in "an almost voluptuous half-light"
("un demi-jour presque voluptueux"). All these prelates,
it seems, are endowed with a highly refined taste for
good eating. Let us remember this simple sketch of the
cardinal whose name we have just cited: "with a weary
look, (he) blessed him with his right hand, while he
squeezed the peaches in the basket with the left" ("d'un
air las, [il] le bénissait de la main droite, pendant
que de la gauche il tâtait des pêches dans la corbeille").
Similarly, the archbishop who is described in *The Sacrilege* is shown at table; he also calls his confessor a
fanatic who seems to him to be too fervent and laughs in
the face of the sacrilegious priest. Let us add to this
series of cardinals or archbishops the cardinal Riccotini,
in *The Poet Assassinated*--comical,ambiguous,a cleric who
tries to caress the young woman who, through his intervention, is asking the pope for an audience, and a cleric
who dares to voice about her a crude play on words.

The most colorful of these ecclesiastics, worthy of
becoming a cardinal and even a pope, is the Reverend
Father Benedetto Orfei, a Benedictine of quality, a heresiarch of genius. Everything in him is rare and excessive: his gluttony (from which he may die) and his lewd-
ness, but also his ascetic practices, which are well able

to reinforce his sensuality, as Apollinaire suggests: "Mysticism is very close to eroticism" ("le mysticisme touche de près l'érotisme"), or again: "the heresiarch was like all men, for all are at the same time sinners and saints, when they are not criminals and martyrs" ("hérésiarque était pareil à tous les hommes, car tous sont à la fois pécheurs et saints, quand ils ne sont pas criminels et martyrs"). We began with a prelate from *The Lectern (Le Lutrin)*, and we end with a strange being who is quasi-diabolical both in his sacrilegious obsessions and in his blasphemies:

> It was known that the Holy Ghost had one day raped a sleeping virgin. This indecent assault had been the work of the Holy ghost, from which Jesus was born...[19]

This heretic, the inventor of a new religion, has nothing but scorn for the old one, a religion "decayed"("pourrie")--always this revealing term--"too old, and which the pope was afraid to touch for fear it would crumble" ("trop vieille, et que le Pape craignait de toucher de peur qu'elle ne s'écroulât'). What words can we attribute to Guillaume Apollinaire himself? The latter, assuredly, which are repeated in *Infallibility* and in many of the stories and poems. But perhaps the former also. And the heresiarch who still believes in God is replaced in *Infallibility* by an apostate who has lost the faith contradicted by science.

The story of *Infallibility* takes place during the "modernism" crisis and seems to have been inspired by an Italian novel, Fogazzaro's *Il Santo*, the translation of which had appeared in 1905 in the *Revue des Deux-Mondes*. Apollinaire's story is dated 1906 and borrows several traits from its predecessor. However, whereas Fogazzaro's hero wanted to reform the church from within in order to restore it to its original form, Apollinaire's hero has lost his faith and wants to bring Catholicism down. André Fonteyne is right in feeling in these pages the vibration of a singular accent, a particular virulence, and perhaps the expression of a personal bitterness. Let us quote a few of these lines:

> I have lost my faith and I am convinced that it cannot stand up to an honest examination by any

man. There is no branch of science that does not
contradict the so-called truths of religion by irrefutable facts.[20] (HC, p. 72)

At the bottom of ecclesiastical hierarchy, monks and
priests, as Apollinaire sees them, perhaps preserve their
faith, but it is a faith of fanaticism, superstition, nar-
rowness of mind. Under their cassocks or robes they are
hiding instincts that cause them to fall back into the
ranks of ordinary men; they are lewd, or at least indul-
gent to things of the flesh. Such is the priest from
Lyons, "stubborn in his faith, thinking that everything
is permitted for the coming of the kingdom of God" ('têtu
dans la foi, pensant que tout est permis pour que le
règne de Dieu arrive"), who, after a night of prayer,
goes and makes an obscene gesture under the windows of
his penitent parishioner. This story, *Of a Monster in
Lyons or Envy (D'un monstre à Lyon ou l'envie)*, has a
Rabelaisian flavor, but it makes one think of a more ir-
reverent and quasi-Voltairian Rabelais. The curé of the
story *The Otmika* shows indulgence for sins of love and
so grants absolution before the sin is committed:

> In your place, Omer, I should commit this sin. Be
> heroic but ask for God's forgiveness before and
> after. As for me, I shall absolve you when you
> come to confession.[21]

However, it must be recognized that this is a sympathetic
priest, the herald of a religion of joy. He preaches
that dancing is good by relying on the fact that Jesus
may have danced at the wedding of Cana. As for monks,
they are uniformly considered as objects of derision.
One such is Father Seraphin: sacrilegious because of
his stupidity and thus a formidable devil's advocate.
So as to increase the divine presence in the Eucharist,
he consecrates all the bread he can find and then re-
alizes, but too late, the disastrous consequences of his
gesture, which has been caused by a quasi-magical faith
in the efficacy of sacramental works. He leaves the convent, volunteers into the Foreign Legion, and dies in
front of Peking.

Another unfrocked priest--at least for a while--is a
young monk from the monastery of Laghet, near Nice. Moved
by the illness of a young girl whom he had formerly loved

and who comes to beg the Virgin to restore her health,
he waits, like all pilgrims, for a miracle that does not
occur. On the contrary, the poor girl dies. The young man
raises his fist toward heaven with the cry: "Christian
brothers, the world is poorly made! ("Frères chrétiens,
le monde est mal fait!") He then reenters the cloisters
forever. He is resigned. He is no longer trying to understand. He is separated forever from a bad world. And
he has lost, it would seem, the candor of his faith as a
novice.

In the story of *The Poet Assassinated* the scene takes
place at Prunn, in a Benedictine monastery that no longer
preserves much of the atmosphere of prayer and meditation
desired by Saint Benedict. On the walls of the refec-
tory, one could see Biblical frescoes, as is the rule,
but they were executed in the manner of cabaret paintings:
Gideon's soldiers in strange postures, suffering from
colic, and "Noah's sex nicely painted, *The Wedding at
Cana* showed a Mannekenpis pissing wine into kegs, while
the bride, at least eight months pregnant, was presenting her stomach as big as a barrel to someone who was
writing on it with charcoal: Tokay."[22] This would seem
to be nothing more than Rabelaisian joking, but the following details go much further into the realm of profanation: the monastery garden is an "earthly paradise,"
filled with love souvenirs; one can indeed hear the singing of the "Vexilla regis prodeunt," but also the love
murmur of thousands of embracing couples; this cloister,
a place of ill repute: "Tycho Brahé made love there in
the past with a pretty Jewess...I have seen the archduke
such and such have fun there with a pretty young boy..."
("Tycho Brahé y fit l'amour autrefois avec une jolie
juive...j'y ai vu l'archiduc un tel s'y amuser avec un
joli garçon"). A strange monastery whose inhabitants
can hardly be considered saints despite the Father Superior's affirmations: "As for me, as you must see, with
my spectacles and my big stomach, I am a saint" ("Moi-
même, tel que vous me voyez, avec mes lorgnons et mon
gros ventre, je suis un saint"). Like Benedetto Orfei,
like all the prelates described by the narrator of *The
Heresiarch and Co.*, these monks are at the same time
gluttons and saints, and their table, sumptuously laden,
is described with complacency. One can understand how

the hero of the story, Croniamantal, can thank his hosts
for their hospitality. He seemed to like this kind of
convent, which resembled the Abbey of Thélème rather than
the Abbey of Solesme: "I shall always remember with
pleasure the simplicity, the gaiety, the freedom which
reign here" ("Je garderai toujours un bon souvenir de la
simplicité, de la gaîte, de la liberté qui règnent ici").
Pleasant eupheuisms! Thus, cloisters as well as pres-
bytaries, episcopal palaces as well as the Vatican, hide
"decay" ("de la pourriture"), just as the Cathedral of
Cologne does, if one believes the picture presented by
Apollinaire, and all would need, to recall the words of
Bernanos, a cleaning of gigantic proportions.

But Apollinaire does not much believe ·in such a purification. His anticlericalism does not express a desire
to·bring down the screens that churchmen place between God
and men. It is founded on a more radical scorn of réli-
gion, which is criticized in its very sources, and first
of all in the Holy Scriptures.

Two stories from *The Heresiarch and Co.,* belonging to
the literary genre of Biblical paraphrase in prose, are
presented as stories "in the manner of" the Gospel and
continue a chapter of the New Testament or of the Acts of
the Apostles. But while *Simon Magus* does not have any
sarcasm, *The Dancer (La Danseuse)* shows a desecrating
type of irony, well worthy of a Voltaire or an Anatole
France. This story is a very short appendix to the story
of John the Baptist; the narrator gives attention to each
of the characters of the bloody drama alluded to by St.
Mark and St. Matthew, but he does so by degrading them,
passing from a sacred tone to a trivial one. John the
Baptist, the legendary figure of the intransigent ascetic,
is nothing more than an "eater of grasshoppers" ("mangeur
de sauterelles") who "invites men to take baths" ("invite
les hommes à prendre des bains"). This might seem only
ridiculous, but there is more! Contrary to the evangel-
ists, Apollinaire endows him with "carnal desires...for
the woman who wanted him" ("désirs charnels...pour celle
qui le voulait"), and makes him jealous of Herod Antipas.
Herodias is a woman who "wants" a man, falls in love--
depraved taste!--with "the seductive leanness of the
penitent" ("la maigreur ragoûtante du pénitent"), and,
with an ultimate touch of sadism, "ardently kisses the
purplish lips of the emaciated Baptist" ("baise ardem-

ment les lèvres violâtres du Baptiste décollé"). Herod
is transposed into the bey of Tunis and Salome into a
dancing rider, the "damnable dance," the "obscene round."
In short, the story, so popular, so often depicted by
painters, musicians, cineasts, is here treated as a parody.

But this is not simply a literary game, and *The Dancer*
is but a wing of a triptych entitled *Three Stories of
Divine Punishment (Trois histoires de châtiments divins)*.
The theme of the scenes is identical: three sinners before God, each guilty of the sin of the flesh (a homosexual, a lewd dancer, an impious husband), are punished
by means of their very sins, according to the law of retaliation: "It pleased God to punish the sins by the
law of retaliation" ("Il plut à Dieu de punir par la
peine du talion les péchés"). The homosexual dies im-
paled, Salome is the victim of her damnable dance, the
skeptical husband has a son who is a hermaphrodite:
three grotesque punishments. Apollinaire himself admitted, in a letter to Madeleine, that this ensemble was
"rather disgusting" ("assez dégoûtant") (TCS, p. 103),
but he published it nonetheless. Even if he only wanted
to have fun, even if the blasphemy were involuntary, it
bursts out just the same and reaches the Christian God--
this jealous God who avenges himself like a man, the
God of the Decalogue, the God-policeman whose colossal
anger is provoked and whose sanctions are automatically
aroused by infractions to the code, particularly the ones
dealing with the flesh: is this not the face of the Christian God as it appeared (sometimes) to the young pupil of
the Marianist Fathers?

The parody of the evangelical tale of the Passion of
Christ that we find in the story of *The Latin Jew* is less
virulent, less significant, more gratuitous. A monstrous
assassin, Gabriel Fernisoun, dies in the street and receives baptism in extremis. His death is surrounded by
miracles. The two policemen who take him to the police
station play the role of the two thieves who were on
either side of Jesus on the Calvary:

> Moreover, one of the two policemen who carried the
> body to the station had laughed, thinking that he
> was dealing with a drunk. He died the next day of
> aneurism. The second one had wiped with his hand-

kerchief the foam that appeared on the lips of the
dying man, then he had closed his eyes. He has
just come into an inheritance that has made him rich
for the remainder of his life...[23]

Thus, the second policeman is the embodiment of the
good thief as well as of the woman who, according to
tradition, wiped the face of Christ with a cloth. The
grotesque parody has a lesson identical to that of the
Three Stories of Divine Punishment: God rewards the
good and punishes the bad, and he does it in an immedi-
ate, tangible, material manner--always an arbitrary and
cruel God. It is true that the narrator does not believe in these miracles, and least of all at the moment
when he claims that they are true: "The two miracles
involving the policemen are obvious" ("Les deux miracles
accomplis sur les agents sont patents"). It is a beautiful example of Voltairian irony, reinforced by a pseudo-
condemnation of a natural explanation: "The science that
tries to explain by natural means the good odor emanat-
ing from a dead body is ridiculous" ("La science est ridicule qui essaye d'expliquer par des moyens naturels
la bonne odeur exhalée par un corps mort").

Another example of a miracle, but without reference to
God this time, and another example of an allusion to the
Gospel, can be found in the story of *The Serviette of the
Poets (La Serviette des poètes)*, with its napkin that
bears the imprint, not only of one single face, like
Veronica's cloth, but of four friends: "and this Saint
Veronica, with her quadruple look, was urging them to
flee on the borders of art to the confines of life" ("et
cette Sainte-Véronique, de son quadruple regard, leur
enjoignait de fuir sur la limite de l'art, aux confins
de la vie"). What seems to have struck the narrator in
Veronica's legend is not so much the compassionate gesture of a woman as the process of a magical reproduc-
tion of a face.

Apollinaire's skepticism is directed against the legends taken from the Bible more often than it is against
the Biblical text itself, and one might suspect in this
an attempt to discredit the Bible indirectly through its
imitations--a procedure that we know was dear to Voltaire. However, in the story of *The Rose of Hildesheim
or the Treasures of the Magi (La Rose de Hildesheim ou*

les trésors des rois mages) Apollinaire establishes a
clear distinction between the canonical and very sober
text of Saint Matthew and the apocryphal writings that
have embellished and denatured it:

> One Sunday in January, as he (the hero of the story)
> had gone to sermon, the pastor spoke of the sages
> of the Orient who came to visit Jesus in the man-
> ger. He cited the verse from the Gospel of St.
> Matthew wherein nothing is said as to the number
> and condition of the pious personages who brought
> gold, incense, and myrrh to Jesus...[24]

The lines that follow this passage could well be entitled: how a myth is born, or how the cult of saints is
propagated. It is a debauchery of the imagination that
embroiders on the original data; it is a veritable fantasmagoria:

> The following days, Egon could not prevent himself
> from thinking about these sages of the Orient whom,
> although he was a Protestant, he imagined, accord-
> ing to Catholic legend, to be crowned and three in
> number: Gaspard, Balthasar, and Melchior...the as-
> trologers whose bones the Cathedral of Cologne takes
> pride in possessing...[25]

These words, in spite of and because of their hyper-
bolical tone, are reminiscent of the mocking tone of *The
Dome of Cologne* ("You are hiding the decay of the Magi"
("Tu recèles la pourriture des rois mages"). This time
the criticism could be endorsed by the most orthodox of
Bollandists. But Apollinaire goes further; he no longer
believes in holiness; for him, holiness can only be an
imposture. A story from *The Poet Assassinated* entitled
Saint Adorata could well have as a subtitle: how to
fabricate a saint or a false saint, and it recalls Anatole France in both its theme and its style. A man has
lost his young mistress and has embalmed her body, which
is taken for the remains of a Christian martyr and is an
object of the veneration of the faithful. The same process occurs in *The Latin Jew* where a sadistic criminal is
going to be canonized because of pseudomiracles that
have occurred at his death, and in the story *Giovanni
Moroni,* where a puller of teeth uses the teeth of his

clients for the edification of the people: "Since then,"
the author writes, "I have thought that these teeth were
probably and very justly becoming venerated relics"("Depuis, j'ai pensé que ces dents devenaient probablement
et très justement des reliques vénérées"). Finally, in
The Sacrilege, Father Seraphin, a famous devil's advocate in canonization trials, has an easy time proving
that all saintliness is suspect: "He despised all the
saints, realizing that they would not have become saints
if he had fulfilled his functions at the time of their
canonization trials" ("Il méprisait tous les saints, se
rendant compte qu'ils ne l'eussent point été, s'il eût
rempli son office à l'époque de leur procès de canonisa-
tion"). The storyteller of *The Heresiarch and Co.* resembles Father Seraphin in this respect, and one could
not find a more clever and earnest devil's advocate; even
his insistence in profanating everything that might appear to be sacred could be considered satanic.

Indeed, what relentlessness in mocking every belief,
in denying every miracle, in extenuating every sacrament!
The person who constantly and radically demolishes sacredness can indeed be called sacrilegious. We have already noted that the plot of *The Latin Jew* deals with
the sacrament of baptism, considered as a formula and
rite that act *ex opere operato*: "This Gabriel Fernisoun
is certainly in paradise," one of the author's friends
--a priest--says to him, "baptism has washed off all his
sins" ("Ce Gabriel Fernisoun est certainement en paradis. Le Baptême l'a lavé de tous ses péchés"). The only
doubt that one might have concerns the liquid used in the
sacrament: if the baptismal water was not pure--and
here one fears that it was nothing other than horse urine
(sic)--the Latin Jew was never baptized! The same type
of automatism can be noted about another sacrament, that
of confession. A monk and a bishop resort to it in the
following manner: "Give me confession, Monseigneur, he
said, and then I shall confess you. They gave each other absolution" ("Confessez-moi, Monseigneur, dit-il, je
vous confesserai ensuite. Ils s'absolvirent mutuelle-
ment"), which is indeed a bit too easy! Too easy, equally, to recite a formula on any kind of bread so that it
may become the body of Christ. Thus the story *The Sacrilege* attacks the dogma of transubstantiation, or at

least its schematic and distorted reduction, for the author seems to forget that true intention and purity of conscience are required for the sacramental gestures to be valid.

It is perhaps in the story of *The Piedmontese Pilgrims (Les Pèlerins piémontais) that the impression of sacrilege* is the strongest, for here the mockery is replaced by a more serious, icy, and definite tone. The young Wilhelm had gone up to Notre-Dame de Laghet several times --a favorite excursion of the Marianist Fathers of Monaco. Moreover, the inhabitants of Nice frequently went up there for walks. He describes with verve and precision people and things and especially the curious ex-votos of popular piety. Then he focuses his attention on the Virgin of Laghet, a vain idol that the pilgrims implore in vain: it is nothing but a "doll,...the prodigious and honorable semblance is nothing else" ("poupée,...le simulacre prodigieux et honorable n'est pas autre chose"), which can be translated as: it does not correspond to any reality. And the continuation of the story proves it, with its vain expectation of a miracle, the malediction of a desperate priest "raising his fist toward the very blue sky, he cried out: Christian brothers, the world is poorly made!" ("levant son poing vers le ciel très bleu, il s'écria: frères chrétiens, le monde est mal fait!" André Fonteyne has well defined this tone as "rather devoid of passion [which Apollinaire uses] in order to illuminate with a strangely murky light the scenes of horror and of blasphemy that animate the story of *The Piedmontese Pilgrims*."

We have examined up to now only the signed works published by Apollinaire. For the sake of completeness, one should mention the numerous works published clandestinely and the team-novels written by René Dalize and attributed to Guillaume Apollinaire: *The End of Babylon (La Fin de Babylone), The Rome of the Borgias (La Rome des Borgia), The Three Don Juans (Les trois don Juan).* In these works, a considerable role is given to religious matters, which are used as a spice for eroticism (or pornography). Sadism likes to attack religion, and many Biblical quotes play on double meanings, most of which are obscene. Basing ourselves only on the two novels published under

Apollinaire's name, it is curious to note their many sim-
ilarities in tone to *The Heresiarch and Co.*, but more
accentuated. Thus, some monks' punishments, like those
in the *Three Stories of Divine Punishment*, are rooted in
their very sins. The narrator lingers complacently on
the orgies of the cardinals of the Roman court and the
equivocal relations between Alexander VI Borgia and his
daughter, depicting all these prelates surrendering to
debauchery between two pious prayers. A year later, in
1914, *The End of Babylon* includes an ample and diverse
paraphrase of the Bible, some chapters of which are translated almost literally. The main part is the story of
the "chaste Suzannah," a spicy tale as presented by the
author, but the most scabrous passages of the Scriptures
are presented with complacency. One could think of it
as a huge joke by a bunch of friends, just as one could
say that Apollinaire's stories are the work of an artist
who is having fun at the expense of his characters but
does not pretend in any way to offer a message or present
a personal position about life or the hereafter.

And the blasphemous intent is certainly less constant,
less pronounced, less virulent than in Jarry or, later,
in André Breton. Often, as André Fonteyne has demonstrated, "as soon as Apollinaire deals with religious
matters," one hesitates to define his intentions. Innocent mockery or serious ideas? Whatever the case may be,
one cannot challenge a certain image of God, of Christianism, of the clergy that emanates from the works about
which we have just spoken and that forms the essential
part of his prose: a tyrannical God, religions--Judaism
as well as Catholicism--that are "putrefying" ("pourris-
santes"), in both senses of the word, that is, dying and
perverting everything around them, men and life. Faith
does not exist; or rather, if anyone believes, it is because of stupidity. This faith is nothing other than
superstitious belief; this religion, when it is not pure
hypocrisy, is nothing other than magic, a collection of
formulas, of sesames, easy to know and so much the more
effective because they deal with uncontrollable realms.
Say a few words and everything is changed: bread becomes
the body of Christ, Paradise opens to the most sadistic
of criminals. That, or else faith is nothing more than
a delirium of the imagination, which embroiders on a few

sentences of the Scriptures and edifies the legend of
the Magi. Worse yet, it is idolatry, the adoration of
ordinary objects such as, for instance, a statue that
is believed to be endowed with a miraculous power. "What
does it matter to the believer," says Apollinaire, "faith
is blind!" ("Qu'importe au croyant, la foi est aveugle!").
    But is this the true faith? The strange universe that
fills the collection of *The Heresiarch and Co.* with its
hideous mass--"monstrous Vatican!"--seems to be the distorted reflection of a Christian universe such as we know
it, a universe made of weaknesses, to be sure, but also
of greatness, a universe peopled with sinners but also
with saints--a dark and ghostly shadow of a reality where
the light streams from the shadows. From *The Putrescent
Magician* to *The Heresiarch and Co.*, from *The Hermit* to
The Dome of Cologne, we see nothing but false saints,
false priests, false beliefs--in other words, heresies--
and never the true faith, real saints, orthodox doctrine.
Apollinaire prefers, as Claude Roy points out, the here-
siarchal theologians to St. Thomas. It is his right, and
the choice allows for more strange or comic effects. We
do not deny its artistic value in any way; we are trying merely to define the attitude that prompted such a
choice, such a consistent preference. Claude Roy thinks
that the narrator of *Simon Magus* knows the Cabala better than the Bible. This hardly seems right to us, but
it is true that the Bible, according to Apollinaire, is
a travestied Bible, a Bible strangely emptied of its
spiritual message, and reduced to marvelous and fantas-
magorical legends (the inalienable heritage of childhood?) or to the most carnal scenes, a truncated Bible,
or else one enriched by the traditions of the Cabala
and the apocrypha.

    What does the creation of such a universe presuppose?
An obsession that one has difficulty in shedding; a bitterness against the religion of one's childhood; a desire to avenge oneself on what has made one suffer, whether
one was subjected to it by force or had adhered to it
with a trusting soul? The story of *Giovanni Moroni* had
already suggested the secret wound made in the heart of
an innocent child by the scandalous spectacle of lewd
monks; is this the origin of an anticlericalism more bitter than that of *La Calotte*?[26]

God is dead and deservedly so; it was necessary to kill
him in order to be able to live and be liberated. But
can one be certain that he is really dead? Some vestiges
--cumbersome, embarrassing, threatening--remain: those
who call themselves his ministers, those who boast about
representing him. They are the ones who should be killed
so that God, the nightmare who haunts our lives, can finally, definitively, die. For, after all, if Apollinaire
were completely freed from the burden of his childhood,
why wouldn't he forget, simply and completely, these religious matters about which he speaks so much? He claims
to dislike unwholesomeness, and he says this with regard
to *The Heresiarch and Co*. Even so, as A. Fonteyne notes:
"as if by chance, it is about religious matters that Apollinairian malice seems to like to be exercised the most,"
and it is in this connection that eroticism is introduced. For De Sade, as we know, eroticism is an act of
militant atheism. To explore, in all directions and
against the seemingly natural order of things, the pos-
sibilities of sexual enjoyment, is to rise up against a
God who incarnates moral order. In Apollinaire's predi-
lection for "the divine Marquis," in his willingness to
plunge into the forbidden section of the Bibliothèque
Nationale,[27] can one not see the same type of quasi-
sacrilegious step, the will to go beyond into excesses,
in order to avenge oneself, it would appear, on a restraint that seemed to be frustrating the instincts?

3

Mourning a Dead God

"Where is the God of my youth"
The Brasier

("Où est le Dieu de ma jeunesse"
Le Brasier)

Apollinaire is never totally free from the hold of religion. Even--and especially--when he degrades it through irony or virulent sarcasm, this very attraction for profanation seems to prove that the umbilical cord was not completely cut.

But sometimes this attachment becomes visible in a positive way, and, subsequent to the loss of his faith when at the lycée of Nice, nostalgia for a dead God emerges more than once. We can discover these traces--quite rare, quite tenuous, but real--during the course of the years whose essence will be encompassed in *Alcools*. Next to the Voltairian storyteller, there is a pure poet, and this is the only one of his faces that Guillaume wants to be preserved: "I am only a poet not Voltairian at all" ("Je ne suis qu'un poète pas voltairien du tout") (letter to Toussaint Luca, May 11, 1908). At the same time that he is writing the stories of *The Heresiarch and Co.* and the pornographic novels, he has a more secret life. He goes through crises, such as his break with Annie Playden, which by his own account seems to have been more than the simple end of a love affair, but was, rath-

er, the end of the world. Metaphysical anxiety seems to
emerge at this point, and even what one might call religious anxiety. Thus we find André Salmon's judgment of
his friend too categorical: "His soul was wholesomely
pagan; he never had the notion of sin." Let us overlook
the wholesomeness of this pagan: we shall have to talk
about it in reference to his relationship with Lou in
1915, when his carnal paganism will explode; but as for
sin, the poet speaks about it well before *Zone*, the poem
of confession.

From his very first attempts at poetry, a poem like *Vae
Soli* can suggest a confidence that may be a confession:

> Alas have come at an evil time
> Diogenes the cynic with Onan
> The old book is a lascivious woman and it cries
> With hot desire with you now...[1] (PW, p. 519)

Can one not detect here a sort of feeling of shame concerning sterile sexual enjoyment? At any rate, nothing
is triumphant here, and this is the final impression that
prevails upon reading *The Hermit*, which is sacrilegious
but desperate, and *The Thief*. These two poems, even if
they express bitterness against Christianism, betray at
the same time a regret at the failure of a dream of purity. The thief himself dares to proclaim that he is a
Christian, and the pagans laugh at him; but he remains
forever marked with the "sign of the cross."

Sometimes, it is necessary to look for this feeling of
sin in a rough draft, crossed out and eventually dis-
carded. Such is the case for the poems of *The Door (La
Porte)*, for several poems written at the Santé, and for
Zone. The poet became ashamed of these confessions, but
even if he renounced them as soon as he made them, he
had made them. The first draft of *The Door* was:

> I have taken my sin from you my mother and now
> I want to suffer and condemning myself...
> (Je t'ai pris mon péché ma mère et maintenant
> Je veux suffrir et que moi-même condamnant...)

We have already suggested that this sin was that of
lust transmitted by a passionate mother to her child;
the reference, it must be admitted, is hasty and remains
elusive.

During the love story that develops between the poet and Annie Playden, the shame of sin comes up several times. Not only because of the origins of the young English girl (she was a puritan's daughter and rather militant in her faith; as soon as she had arrived in Neu-Glück, where she was to be a tutor, she opened a Sunday school--let us understand by that a sort of Protestant catechism class) but also because if to yield to love was sinful for her, it was also sinful for Guillaume. Annie appears to him as a malefic sorceress whose eyes seduced him and condemned him to hell: he "burns in these flames" like the bishop of *The Lorelei*. One might think that the latter poem is a simple imitation of the German poet Brentano. But another piece dedicated to this love affair has a suggestive line that must be taken at its fullest sense: "One knows very well that one is damning oneself" ("On sait très bien que l'on se damne"), he says in *The Gipsy (La Tzigane)*. Let us recognize here, with Marie-Jeanne Durry, a confession of carnal passion judged to be evil. Why? Because the lovers do not love each other in a natural manner and they search for pleasure by cheating:

> Love heavy like a trained bear
> Danced standing up when we wanted
> And the blue bird lost its feathers
> And the beggars their Ave...[2] (PW, p. 99)

The next line: "One knows very well that one is damning oneself" thus betrays the clear consciousness of the immoral, guilty, satanic character of their too carnal love--a marvelous, exalting love, and yet one that is considered to be bad.

The famous *Song of the Poorly Loved* is related to *The Gipsy* on this score, since in it there is a question of "regrets on which hell is founded" ("regrets sur quoi l'enfer se fonde..."). Regrets of too carnal a flame, of forbidden kisses, perhaps even of having perverted the young, hitherto innocent, English girl. This "old serpent" that is dancing on the poet's "dead gods," is it not his evil genie, his guilty sensuality? The new God who has chased the old ones away is an offspring of the devil who has us in his hold, who leads us by the fatality of sin. This explains the following stanza, admir-

able in its lucidity and despair, consecrating the loss
of freedom:

> The demons of chance according to
> The song of the firmament are leading us
> With lost sounds their violins
> Are making the human race dance
> Backwards on the way down...[3] (PW, p. 58)

The Song--as S.I. Lockerbie was the first to point out
--recounts a metaphysical drama: the quest for the absolute; it tells of a futile wandering. As Lockerbie
says "The loss of love at the beginning of the poem prepares the spiritual disorder at the end." One can explain the nature of this disorder, or at least note that
it is due to the loss of the faith of childhood, to un-
faithfulness towards God. Let us therefore take seriously the main stanza of *The Song*, which decries the
death of the gods (but the God of childhood is cited
among them):

> Many of these gods have perished
> It is for them that the willows weep
> The great Pan the love Jesus Christ
> Are indeed dead and the cats are miaowing
> In the courtyard I am weeping in Paris...[4]

The great carnal Pan and the spiritual Christ are equal
in death, and the former was not able to triumph over
the latter. Only the satanic serpent is reigning: "god
of my gods which have died in autumn" ("dieu de mes dieux
morts en automne").

The same tone of deep melancholy, caused by a similar
drama, can be seen in *One Evening (Un Soir)*, which can
probably be dated 1904. In it, the suffering for love
lost is alluded to by a sculptural reference to the Passion of Christ on Calvary, a Passion that unfolds backwards, for the last verses speak of Palm Sunday while
the preceding lines depicted the death of the renegade
apostle and the soldiers throwing dice for the vestments
of Christ. One hesitates to identify the actors of this
strange scene: "A phantom has committed suicide....The
apostle is hanging from the fig tree and slowly salivates"
("Un fantôme s'est suicidé....L'apôtre au figuier pend
et lentement salive"). Who is this unfaithful one? The

woman who has left the poorly loved? The poorly loved himself, unfaithful to his God--because of this bad love. It is a poem marking, above all, the end of love, but it is a religious poem because of its evangelical framework and some of its cries, which one could call prayers, such as the first stanza:

> An eagle descended from this sky white with angels
>   And you sustain me
> Will you let all these lamps tremble for long
>   Pray pray for me...[5] (PW, p. 126)

A few lines of the draft foreshadowed the atmosphere of *Zone*, for in them the picture of the Calvary became broader, more modern: "And some poor modern people in the background flee" ("Et des pauvres modernes au dernier plan s'enfuient").

Finally, a line that was not published defines perfectly the poet's tone in this poem, as well as in the large poems of *Alcools* and especially *Zone*: "You should into your voice place hell and shadow" ("Il faudrait dans ta voix mettre l'enfer et l'ombre").

Christ does not appear in this evocation of the Calvary, in which the eye is held by a few secondary details: the roads strewn with palms, the hanged Judas, the soldiers playing with dice. But isn't He felt in this very absence or as a veiled presence to which the initial invocation "Pray pray for me" is addressed? It is impossible to affirm this, and one can accept an erotic interpretation of the poem that would in no way exclude the interpretation we have just given.

After 1904, the poet goes through a period of sterility of which two large poems of 1907-1908 reveal the secret: *The Brasier (Le Brasier)* and *The Betrothal (Les Fiançailles)*. There again, the regret for a dead God--for the Christian God and no longer the pagan gods--can be felt in a few lines, a few words. Such is the case at the very beginning of *The Brasier*:

> Where are the heads I held
> Where is the God of my youth
> Love has become bad...[6] (PW, p. 108)

It seems difficult not to admit that this God is Jesus Christ, contrary to what R. Lefèvre says when he asso-

ciates this divinity with love.[7] Let us note, at any
rate, the constant connection in *Alcools* between the end
of a love and the end of faith, from *The Song* to *Zone*.
Let us also point to the reference, in *The Betrothal* as
well as in *One Evening*, to the drama of the Calvary,
which is introduced to express the poet's suffering. No
derision, but an indirect and unvoluntary homage to the
exemplary character of the Passion of Christ--as later
in *Zone:*

> An angel has exterminated during my sleep
> The sheep the shepherds of the sad sheepfolds
> False centurions carried off
>   the vinegar...[8] (PW, p. 129)

Just as in *The Putrescent Magician*, the Scriptures are
taken in reverse; false centurions follow false magi;
what is derisory is the poet's suffering in relation to
that of Christ--facing that of Christ. One word, and
only one, the first word of the draft of *The Betrothal*,
was addressed to the God of youth:

> (Lord)
> I no longer even have mercy for myself...
> (Seigneur)
> Je n'ai plus même pitié de moi...

Other Biblical references came naturally to the poet
who had wanted to give to his confidence a quasi-religious
tone: "I meditate divinely...I observe the day of rest
on Sunday" ("Je médite divinement...j'observe le repos
du dimanche"). It is again in this poem that his forgotten, betrayed, misguided youth emerges like a regret:

> I have had the courage to look back
> The cadavers of my days
> Mark my path and I cry for them
> Some are decaying in Italian churches...[9] (PW,p.131)

Churches of Rome, where Angelica must have taken the
little Wilhelm during the festivities of Christmas or of
the Befana, Santa Maria Maggiore or San Vito--the baptismal site--chapels of the schools of Monaco or Cannes,
where the adolescent took his first communion and spent
a night in prayer--they now hold nothing more than moribund memories, which the poet is bemoaning.

We note here the fleeting appearances of a regret,
which will become explicit in the years 1911-1912, without forgetting that during this period Apollinaire writes
other books and works on the publication of the *Oeuvre*
of the Marquis de Sade, among other things. In poetry,
he finishes the portrayal of a gallery of animals that
will be collected in *The Bestiary (Le Bestiaire)*, but
some of which had appeared in *The Phalange*. A formal
work, a divertisment, spiritual poetry, *The Bestiary* is
all that, but it betrays, under its humorous mask, a
deeper confidence than would appear on the surface. Can
it not be guessed in the following lines?

> God! I am going to be twenty-eight years old
> Years poorly lived, by my will? (PW, p. 13)
> (Dieu! je vais avoir vingt-huit ans
> Et mal vécus, à mon envie?)

Two texts catch our attention: the quatrain of *The Ox*
(Le Boeuf) and that of *Orpheus* dedicated to fish. In
them one can feel a certain attitude of the poet before
God.

Illustrating Dufy's drawing of a winged ox, here is
the first one:

> This cherub sings the praises
> Of Paradise where, near the angels,
> We shall live again, my dear friends,
> When the good Lord will allow it.[10] (PW, p. 32)

This poem, the last one of the collection, thus ends
on a happy note, on a traditional wish: paradise at the
end of your days, a happy place where friends meet around
a God of kindness and majesty. But, since humor sur-
rounds all the poems of *The Bestiary,* one is tempted to
read this quatrain by stressing its emphatic aspect to
the point of destroying the pious wish: an amusing pir-
ourette. the last "joke" of this mystifier who cannot,
on the evidence, still believe in these fables of heaven
and hell.

Apollinaire, as if he foresaw these diverse inter-
pretations and felt the strangeness of this ending, com-
mented on this quatrain in one of the notes that he added to the collection. In this note, he reinforces by a
lengthy (and heavy?) commentary the hope for immortality

that emerged from the poem:

> Those who practice poetry look for and love noth-
> ing other than the perfection that is embodied in
> God himself. Would this divine kindness, this su-
> preme perfection abandon those whose life's goal
> was to discover them and glorify them? This seems
> impossible to conjecture, and, in my opinion, poets
> have the right to hope for the eternal happiness
> after death that is achieved by the total knowledge
> of God, that is, of sublime beauty.[11] (PW, p. 35)

One might think that one is reading San Juan de la
Cruz or Claudel, poets who feel that all beauty is a reflection of the Supreme Beauty. The style seems borrowed from some pious work, and this is what makes the
poet's sincerity suspect; the bombastic tone is in such
evidence here, not so much with regard to divine poetry
--so divine that it takes the place of God--as with regard to the reference to the God of the Bible evoked by
the cherub in the poem. The thought is orthodox, but the
style throws a doubt on its content. However, nothing
makes one interpretation more valid than another, and
one can be allowed to take Apollinaire at his word. Nothing obligates us to see in *The Ox*, or in its editorial
note, a skeptical intention. At the moment when he no
longer believed either in heaven or hell, Apollinaire
was able to dream of a Christian paradise, was able to
think that his poetry, for want of anything else, would
save him: dreams are sometimes contradictory to the reality of which one believes oneself to be conscious.

These remarks can be applied to another poem from *The
Bestiary*, *Orpheus*, which is dedicated to the God of
youth, to Jesus Christ:

> Let your heart be the bait and heaven the pool!
> For, sinner, what soft or salt water fish
> Can equal, by its shape and taste,
> The beautiful divine fish that is Jesus,
> $\qquad\qquad\qquad$ My Savior?   (PW, p. 20)

What a strange, surprising, unexpected apparition,
that of Jesus under the guise of Orpheus! Dufy followed
the example of the early Christians who saw in the Thra-
cian bard, in the savior of Eurydice descended into hell,

a prefiguration of Jesus the Redeemer, and who had drawn
on the walls of the Roman catacombs a Christ-Orpheus be-
witching the animals with his lyre; it is known that they
liked to scatter drawings of fish, the Greek name of
which was the anagram of that of the Savior. Dufy has
given us the key of his drawing by engraving IXΘYS on
the side of a whale. One can understand what fascinated
Apollinaire in this subject: figures and anagrams, the
unusual parallel between a God and an animal, between
the sacred and the profane. As always, it is the mar-
ginal aspects of religion that attract him. Later, in
1917, he noted a passage of St. Augustine on the same
acrostic, but, as early as in *The Bestiary,* he justifies
the traditional interpretation in an erudite note about
Orpheus: "Created in magic, he learned the future and
predicted, in a Christian manner, the coming of the savior" (PW, p. 33).

Thus Apollinaire tends to confuse religion and magic,
to see in Jesus only a powerful worker of miracles; rather than show admiration, he amuses himself. As in the
note to *The Ox,* an emphatic tone pervades these long alexandrines, which are too noble, too rhythmical. Thus,
a pleasant amusement, but without any degradation, and
different in this respect from the prose tales and from
poems like *The Dome of Cologne.* And if there is a confidence, perhaps it lies in the term "sinner," which the
poet applies to himself. Later, in *Zone,* the same image
of Christ the Savior will emerge, evoked by the fish of
the Mediterranean, a remedy against sin this time sym-
bolized by the "octopi of the deep."

Christ is cited once in the poem of *The Traveller (Le
Voyageur),* a serious poem this time, published in September, 1912, but which must be dated a year or two
earlier--some critics date it 1910. It is already a simultaneous poem, a montage of short independent fragments,
the leitmotiv of which is given by the first two lines
and reappears at the end:

> Open this door for me where I am knocking in tears
> Life is variable as much as Euripos... (PW, p. 78)
> (Ouvrez-moi cette porte où je frappe en pleurant
> La vie est variable aussi bien que l'Euripe...)

Another poem of tears, like *The Song,* like *The Betroth-*

al, but what then is this door that is closed to the
poet, if not that of a lost paradise, that of the famil-
ial home (and the word "orphans" in the main body of the
poem invites such an interpretation), that of a house
forbidden forever. Marie-Jeanne Dury is correct in speaking of the parable of the foolish virgins knocking in
vain at the closed door of the wedding hall, and if one
thinks of the Bible or of the New Testament it is because
a strange line is going to burst out suddenly in the
poem, a touch of color, a strident note, but even more,
a tragic element, a sudden irruption of a dead God, whose
image is not completely forgotten:

> One night I stopped at a sad inn
> Near the Luxembourg
> At the back of the hall there was a Christ
> > flying away
> Someone had a weasel
> Someone else a hedgehog
> People were playing cards
> And you had forgotten me...[13]

As in *The Song*, as in *The Betrothal*, the lover has forgotten the poorly loved who, himself, has forgotten his
God. In the midst of a daily world, among people and
animals, suddenly arises the regret for lost love, lost
faith. A life-size crucifix, like the one of the *Lapin
agile*,[14] a cabaret Christ, a comradely Jesus, a strange
element in the scenery, already a surrealistic, mis-
placed, incongruous object, manifests the intrusion of
the sacred into the world of triviality. But it is not
because of his flaming picturesqueness that this Christ
is flying away, as he will do in *Zone*. The general tone
of the poem invites us to see in this image the expression of a profound feeling. No one is speaking to this
Christ, whose élan captivates the eye; he is "flying
away" ("s'envole"). Perhaps no one--except the poet--
has noticed this, for he is relegated to "the back of the
hall." He is merely there, useless, perhaps mocked by
one of the drinkers, exposed to outrages but present in
his agony and in the tragic stretching of his tortured
body. In this "sad inn" ("auberge triste"), as in Apollinaire's life, he plays the role of the great bronze
Christ in Claudel's play *Hard Bread (Pain dur):* that of

a cumbersome object about which no one cares, an object that one does not know how to get rid of, meaningless, desecratized in appearance--and yet, in the poet's mind a presence that gives meaning, form, and hope to all the painful and desolate scenes that are taking place under his statuelike gaze. Take away this Christ and Apollinaire's poem *The Traveller* will lose something--a religious background that gives another dimension to the personal and sentimental drama of which these lines are the echo.

Before considering the confidences that Apollinaire whispers into the poems of 1911/1912, it is necessary to point out that during these years he was working on a "long novel about the end of the world," a novel that will be transformed and used as the finale of the story of *The Poet Assassinated*. This project seems to mark a change in his manner of looking at religious matters; at least one no longer finds the sarcastic tone of *The Heresiarch and Co*. According to the proposed plan, the action was to center on a persecution directed against Christians in the year 2107. A procession left from the Sacré-Coeur to go to the Conciergerie where the cardinal-archbishop of Paris was imprisoned. The prophet Enoch reappeared on earth, and under the name of Moses Enveh, allowed himself to be massacred by the crowd after denouncing Apollonius Zabath, the Antichrist who was the leader of the persecution. Such a subject seems strange, but is it not connected with that of *The Putrescent Magician*, and is not the antichrist a figure that haunts Apollinaire? Here he seems to be nailing him to the pillory. This is what emerges from *The Poet Assassinated*, a laicized transposition of the initial novel. As in the note to *The Ox*, in *The Bestiary*, Apollinaire proclaims the sacred grandeur of poetry. His hero, the poet Croniamental, dies murdered by a stupid crowd that fails to see the resemblance between its victim and Moses:

I am Croniamantal, the greatest of living poets. I have often seen God face to face. I have borne the divine flash, which was tempered by my human eyes. I have lived eternity. But the time having come, I have come to rise up against you...[15] (PA, p. 112)

Even if he does not believe in it, the narrator here
gives homage to the Bible and leans on its authority to
exalt its poetic task. Perhaps here, as in *The Hills
(Les Collines)*, poetry succeeds religion, but without
discrediting the latter, which was not the case in *The
Heresiarch and Co.*

We finally come to the works in which Apollinaire sings
his encounter with God--rare works, but capital ones:
the poems of *At the Santé (A la Santé)* and *Zone*, which
clarify and reinforce each other, even if the poems of
1911 do not reach the perfection of the most important
of the poems of *Alcools*.

The facts that brought Apollinaire to a cell in the
Santé prison are known. Injustly suspected of receiving
and concealing stolen property and even of having stol-
en the *Mona Lisa*, he will spend a week in jail before
being exonerated. A simple incident but one that will
be the cause of a pathetic upheaval for him. André Salmon, who visited him, saw him helpless and haggard. For
a man who confused his life with poetry, it was natural
that he should confide to paper the feelings that tortured him. It was no longer literature, although vague
reminiscences of Musset and Verlaine might have crossed
his mind. We have the drafts he then wrote, only some
of which were retained in *Alcools*. Why some and not others? First of all because of their poetic value, as was
the case for the poems of *Rhénanes*. The poems of *Alcools*
have a more elaborate form, more restraint, density, and
concision than the drafts--first sketches that were not
finished, notations that were too simple to be transposed
successfully into an artistic form. Indeed, one can
hardly see how to create a real poem from phrases such
as "Poor mommy, My poor brother, Forgive me Forgive me"
("Pauvre maman, Mon pauvre frère, Pardonnez-moi Pardonnez-
moi") or, to come to religious lines: "Virgin sweeter
than sugar, Virgin who have protected me" ("Vierge plus
douce que le sucre, Vierge qui m'avez protégé") It was
too bad a beginning; it came to a short end.

But other verses, other stanzas, that were not at all
unworthy of their author, were also not used by him. For
instance:

     I am Guillaume Apollinaire
     Derived from a slavic name as a true name

> My life is totally sad
> An echo always answers no
> When I say a prayer... 16

This confidence is too direct, and especially too precise; less elaborate than others, it is true, but too revealing, too personal. Apollinaire will be more daring in *Zone*, and at the same time he will keep back a part of himself. Where does this modesty come from? When it is a question of religious feelings, one can find an explanation in *Zone*: "You are ashamed when you catch yourself saying a prayer" ("Vous avez honte quand vous vous surprenez à dire une prière").

The happy *bouc-en-train*17 of Guillaume's gang--according to an expression of Willy--can well pass in his friends' eyes for a pagan of robust health; he carefully hides in his everyday life the nostalgia for a forgotten faith. We were able to detect whiffs of it in some of his poems and more often in the rough drafts--in such or such a line later deleted. He is ashamed to express these feelings, ashamed to confess that he still cares for this "old superstition." But alone in his cell, where he writes to alleviate a heart swollen with pain and anxiety (does he not fear that he will be expelled from France as an undesirable alien, as a pornographic writer?), he is no longer afraid of what people will say and the most simple words come to his pen--the most childish words even, for they correspond perfectly to his religious faith, which has remained literally a childish faith, "the pretty faith of his childhood," as Claudel would say. Gone are the ironic barbs and the Voltairian sarcasms; only a child remains--Angelica's child, the school boy of St. Charles--who transcribes gestures remembered from long ago:

> And I have just said a rosary
> With my fingers as beads
> O Holy Virgin listen to them
> Listen to my poor prayers... 18

What else remained for this lover of a passionate life when he was imprisoned in the four walls of a cell, when the tide of amusements receded, when the flames of lust were extinguished, when the rumors of the city were

silent--but prayer. He could have--one might have expected it--amused himself, imagined new tales, revived
the memories of his loves. But in this borderline situ-
ation, in front of danger, the glamour of the imaginary
disappeared, the whole brilliant facade that was hiding
the depth of his life crumbled, letting the roots of his
existence emerge. This explains his search for identity:

> I am Guillaume Apollinaire
> Derived from a slavic name as a true name...

Doubting himself, discovering his radical relevancy,
the poet is looking for an absolute, but he "has lost
the habit of believing" ("a perdu l'habitude de croire")
--as he will say a year later--and God no longer answers
him. Even so, his prayer has sprung forth, spontaneous-
ly,whether because of weakness or because of an old habit
suddenly recovered does not matter; it *has* sprung forth
and first of all, in the most natural manner, toward the
one who is the most reachable, toward the one who is the
usual intermediary for a Christian between God and men,
toward the Virgin Mary. No need for complicated sentences;   the pain is so deep that the sinner need only
repeat, like a chant that soothes suffering, the Ave
Maria of his rosary; the naïve detail--the counting of
the Aves by tens on his fingers--guarantees the authen-
ticity of his gesture. "Poor?" Indeed these prayers
were poor, and doubly so because they came from the
heart of a wretched man and because he did not know what
to say: "Virgin who have protected me" ("Vierge qui
m'avez protégé").

This line introduces a hope; it has so often been repeated to the pupil of the Marianist Fathers that Mary
was the Protector, the supreme Mother, that he feels,
when he thinks of Her, that he is entering a zone of
calm and security. It is indeed to the Heavens that he
attributes the consolations that he might receive in
prison: his friends' letters.

> I have just received letters
> Thus you are not abandoning me
> Jesus who was emprisoned
> And whom the twelve abandoned...[19]

This is a wholly Christian attitude. The Christian

knows that he is marked with the sign of the cross and
relives in his own existence the very life of his Master,
that he conforms to Jesus, that he suffers with the suffering Jesus, completing in his own flesh, as St. Paul
says, what the passion of Jesus is lacking. It can be
said that these are very grandiloquent terms for Apollinaire, but how can one interpret otherwise these very
simple and yet so Christian lines? The thief of old,
"credulous and red-headed like his Master" ("crédule et
roux comme son Maître"), did not deny the latter; he
finds him again in prison and in isolation, and this
presence is beneficial to him: it allows him to be con-
soled in his turn. In *Zone*, one will find again this
assimilation between the suffering Christ and the unhappy poet.

The following stanza is the most explicit as to this
renewal of faith, as to its quality and its fragility:

I have just found my faith again
Like in the beautiful days of my youth
Lord accept my homage
I believe in you I believe I believe...[20]

The expression of the prayer is stereotyped ("accept
my homage"), but the insistence of the last line marks
an intense desire rather than a certitude. As for Apollinaire's faith, it is not that of an adult, consciously
accepted, constantly nourished and lived; it is not a
flowering certitude like that of a Claudel. It is an
emotional attachment to the Christian God, especially to
the humano-divine Person of Christ and His Mother; it is
a hope in their protection; it is the thought that they
sometimes help us, especially in days of misfortune. It
is a poor faith, as poor as the prayers; it is not a
warming blaze, but a pale glow of cinders. The fire was
smouldering under the embers; it will be able to be re-
vived--and this will create *Zone*--before being extinguished, perhaps forever.

Another prayer, addressed directly to God, will appear
in *Alcools*. It is perhaps less revealing; it is a little
too literary to our taste, too elaborate, too conven-
tional. However, it does express Christian feelings:

How bored I am between these naked walls
Painted with pale colors...
...What will become of me O Lord who knows my pain
You who have given it to me
Have pity on my tearless eyes my pallor
The noise of my chained chair

And all these poor hearts beating in prison
The Love which accompanies me
Have pity especially on my weak reason
And this despair which is invading it.[21] (PW, p. 143)

One thinks of Job's complaints, at least with respect
to the authentically Biblical thought: God, the master
of our lives, gives us the good and the bad and we can
only bless him for it; if the pain seems to be too strong,
one can pray to him to help us bear it. Resignation,
confidence, pleas for help, these feelings are expressed
and concentrated in a miserere twice repeated: "have
pity," and they are enlarged, which is rare in Apollinaire's work (except in *Zone*), to reach a sort of broth-
erly compassion for all sufferers, and first of all the
other prisoners. Only the noble alexandrines, the classical stanza, the slightly mannered terms make us feel
somewhat less, here, the sincere conviction that was
bursting out in the rough drafts. Job transposed into
classical meters loses all his power. To hear the accent and the pain of a suffering man, united in a cry
that is perfectly expressed in the verse of the psalm
writers of Israel, we will have to wait for *Zone*.

A second crisis is going to strike Apollinaire, already shaken by his imprisonment: Marie Laurencin will
leave him in June, 1912, ending their long, often stormy
liaison. This was the very end of this love affair, the
drama of which was divulged in a few poems--*The Mirabeau
Bridge (Le Pont Mirabeau), Marie,* and *Hunting Horn (Cors
de chasse)*. Michel Décaudin says that "*Zone* is the echo
of this trial." This is true, but just as the emotional
drama of *The Song* spread out to such dimensions as the
tragedy of existence, just as the break revealed the very
crack in the universe, and just as one's eyes were raised
from the streets of London or Paris to the far away celestial bodies moving indifferently around our somber

planet Earth, similarly, in this poem, which starts off
with a "heart-rending adieu to a dead love," a whole
life, all of life, the whole universe will be questioned
once again.

Besides this emotional shock, many other trials will
cause Apollinaire to emit the cry embodied in *Zone*. The
most important of them seems to be, in our opinion, his
reading of Blaise Cendrars' poem *Easter (Pâques)*, to
which *Zone* is so close, especially in the first draft,
that it is impossible to think of a chance encounter.
It would be possible to prove how the very composition
of Apollinaire's poem was influenced by that of *Easter*,
how from one state to another everything seems to point
to Apollinaire's wanting to attenuate the possible rap-
prochements. Before all, it seems to us, that upon reading or hearing Cendrars' poem, the poet who the preceding year had let rise toward God some "poor prayers" had
found a frame of mind that was familiar to him. In Cendrars' loneliness--"Now I am alone...Lord I am alone...
Lord I am too much alone" ("Je suis seul à présent...
Seigneur je suis tout seul...Seigneur je suis trop seul")
--he found his own loneliness: "You are alone" ("Tu es
seul"). In Cendrars' prayer and aspirations--"I would
have wished, Lord, to enter into a church" ("J'aurais
voulu entrer, Seigneur, dans une église")--he found his
own prayer and his own aspirations: "...shame is holding you back/From entering a church" ("...la honte te
retient/D'entrer dans une église"). In Cendrars' doubt
--"Perhaps I lack faith" ("peut-être que la foi me manque")
--he found his own doubt:"But I have lost the habit of
believing" ("Mais j'ai perdu l'habitude de croire").
One who did not dare to publish poems that might have
looked like prayers is superseded by a friend who is not
afraid to create a modern poem from a prayer, from a
long monologue to Christ the Lord. One who felt himself
to be the leader of modern poets, the champion of the
avant-garde, is outdistanced by a poet who unites the
Christian religion and the twentieth century, Catholicism
and the modern city. To which can be added the shock he
must have felt upon reading in *Mercure de France*, probably
in September, 1912, Rachilde's account of Marinetti's novel
The Pope's Monoplane (Le Monoplan du Pape). Apollinaire
could find in it a condemnation of Greco-Latin antiquity

and a relationship between the pope and aviation.

But Apollinaire will react with Cendrars' poem in a wholly personal manner, for his circumstances were not those of his friend. While the latter will confess that he had never prayed "when (he) was a little child," the former pupil of the Marianist Fathers will be able to affirm that he "is very pious," and that he has prayed "all night in the school chapel." In the midst of his crisis, exactly as in his cell at the Santé the previous year, he is recovering his faith--and it can only be his childhood faith, for he has no other; but this faith is confronted with the doubts, the exigencies, of a mature man. *Zone* is the poem of recovered faith and of faith quickly lost again, the poem of a conversion soon to be aborted. It is a story as thrilling as the account Claudel makes of his own conversion at Notre-Dame de Paris, on Christmas Day 1886, with the difference that instead of an unprepared document we have a perfect poem. Though we often--constantly--use the first draft of what became *Zone*, we must not forget the literary aspect, the stylistic work that went into the poet's first cry, and our attention is given to this stylistic work as much as to the original cry. But even if this poetic creation, this language, this universe of *Zone* does not correspond to what, in reality, was Guillaume Apollinaire's attitude during this period of his life, it nonetheless expresses his best dreams. The idealization of Christ, for instance, can surprise the faithful reader of the storyteller of *The Heresiarch and Co.* or of the poet of *Palace (Palais)*, but this is not a fantasy, a wish to surprise, or a palinode but rather a submission to an interior feeling that is perhaps more authentic than his daily behavior.

In other words, *Zone* allows us to reach the most authentic Apollinaire--if one is willing to admit the position that Georges Bernanos expressed in the following lines of his *Letter to the English*: "Experience has proved to me, too late, that one cannot explain human beings by their vices, but on the contrary by the purity, the unsulliedness they have kept within, by what remains to them of youth, even if one has to look for it very deeply."[22] *Zone*, the poem of recovered youth--even idealized youth-- thus explains Apollinaire's soul and reveals the heart of a man of thirty-two who is establishing a balance sheet, who is contemplating, and with what trepidation, the very depth of his life. In this respect it is a religious poem, just as a Greek tragedy, a statue of Ligier Richier, Rouault's *Old King*, and Albert Camus' *The Fall* are "religious." Moreover, the allusions to the symbols and writings of a well-defined religion, the Catholic religion, make of it one of the great Christian poems of our literature, equal to a sonnet of *Wisdom (Sagesse)*, a hymn from *Corona benignitatis Anni Dei,* and a *Tapestry (Tapisserie)* by Péguy. Thus, it deserves the careful reading that, forgetting all prejudices, and following the poet's own stride, line after line, will allow a whole significance to emerge.

> Finally you are tired of this ancient world
> (A la fin tu es las de ce monde ancien)

This first movement of the poem is a profession of modernity, yes; but it leads--and critics have neglected to note this--to a homage to religion that becomes actual because of its very eternity:

> Only religion has remained totally new religion
> Has remained simple like the hangars of
>   the airfield
> (La religion seule est restée toute neuve
>   la religion
> Est restée simple comme les hangars de
>   Port-Aviation)

What surprising adjectives: "new" and "simple," this religion that the narrator of *The Heresiarch* and the poet of *The Betrothal* had described as "putrefying"! And why the unexpected comparison with the sheds of an airport-- these new churches? The following lines allow us to understand him better:

> Alone in Europe you are not ancient
>   O Christian faith
> The most modern European is you Pope Pius X
> (Seul en Europe tu n'es pas antique
>   ô Christianisme
> L'Européen le plus moderne c'est vous Pape Pie X)

Statements even more surprising than those of the two

preceding verses. If it were not for the authoritative
tone and the direct accent, one might suspect Apollinaire
of being ironical when he describes as "modern" the pope
who, in 1907, had denounced the "modernistic" error.
Elsewhere, Apollinaire will mock (without spitefulness)
this strict pope, who condemned the tango as lascivious
(he should have recommended the furlane, a Venetian dance,
says the narrator of *The Seated Woman* [*La Femme assise*]:
before being elected pope, Joseph Sarto was a Venetian
patriarch). When, in *The Poet Assassinated*, a married
couple alludes to the white hair of Pius X, it is to bring
out his "antiquity, snow that Catholics think to be eternal, hot-house lily" ("antiquite, neige que les catholiques
pensent éternelle, lys en serre"). Here, no hot-house
eternity but a pope standing at the prow of Europe, in
the great wind churned by the propellers. It is because
this pope had the great merit, in Apollinaire's eyes, of
blessing from the Vatican terrace the French aviator Beaumont, the first winner of the air race between Paris and
Rome, one day in May, 1911. A spectacular gesture, divulged by the papers, which struck the heart of a poet in
love with wings, a man haunted, as has so often been repeated, by the complex of Icarus. A gesture that finally
allowed this former pupil of the Fathers to feel proud of
being a Christian. The thief, the shameful disciple of a
crucified God, of a religion of mourning and "humid moral
flowers," could now raise his head and welcome with the
same élan the inventions of progress and the message of
Christ. And perhaps the salute to the pope was only the
expression of a deeper need, that of coming back to a
vivifying source, to the fountain of youth that faith
could be. The following two lines appeal to the renewal
of the internal being and no longer only to a civilization
that is getting old terribly fast:

> And you whom the windows are watching shame is
> holding you back
> From entering a church for confession this morning
> (Et toi que les fenêtres observent la honte
> te retient
> D'entrer dans une église et de t'y confesser
> ce matin)

A sudden change of tone, passing to a minor mode, a

serious reflecting upon oneself and no longer any enthu-
siasm but fear and trembling. The silhouette of the pope
disappears and the portal of the church remains, peppered
by the looks of the curious. In vain did the poet salute
religion; he well knows that this is not sufficient, and
that an adherence of his whole being is necessary. His
heart is calling for the renewal that confession might
bring, but human respect prevents him from doing it--the
very feeling that held back Paul Claudel for four years
at the threshold of the church of reconciliation. However, this confession cannot remain repressed; it is going to unroll all through the poem, which becomes in turn
a church that will take the appearance of the chapel of
the first communion, that of St. Charles of Monaco. Blaise
Cendrars had already expressed the wish "to enter a
church," but he was not thinking of confession. Apollinaire's wish bears witness to a real Christian feeling,
the feeling of sin that is going to saturate the entire
poem.

For a moment, in a second movement, religion is forgotten. The poet wanders through the streets of the capital, his eyes caught by the lively colors of the "posters that sing aloud" ("affiches qui chantent tout haut"),
his ears assailed by the moaning of the sirens and the
barking of the bells. Why suddenly come back from a street
of Paris in 1912 to "the young street" and to the youth
dressed in "blue and white" if not because the religious
theme necessitates this going back to the sources, to the
"beautiful days of youth," to the time before sin, to the
time of innocent faith, to the time of wonder-filled religion, to the time of triumphant Christ?

> Your mother dresses you only in blue and white
> (Ta mère ne t'habille que de bleu et de blanc)

First image of youth: a vision of ingenuousness sym-
bolized by the colors of Mary: it makes one think of the
lines of *Prayer* (but it is less successful):

> You are very pious and with your oldest friend
>   René Dalize
> You love nothing so much as the pomp of
>   the church...
> (Tu es très pieux et avec le plus ancien de
>   tes camarades René Dalize

Vous n'aimez rien tant que les pompes de
                    l'Eglise...)

We have already defined this youthful religion,founded
on the glory of the Catholic liturgy--the very one that
had seduced Huysmans--and on the élans of sensitivity.
But can one ask anything else of a young child whom one
of his future friends,Hélène d'Oettingen,will later de-
scribe as "dazzled with the striking and many colored infinite of the rites of the Catholic religion"? Cendrars
regretted this outdated pomp:

Where are the long services and where are the
                    beautiful canticles?
(Où sont les longs offices et où les beaux
                    cantiques?)

The former pupil of St. Charles is going to make them
live again after recalling a singular memory, the holy
vigil in the chapel--a memory so precise that it could
not have been invented--that marked the impressionable
child in his most intimate fibers: the hour, the flick-
ering of the gaslight, the precautions taken for a clan-
destine escape. *Zone* is a remembrance of things past
worthy of Marcel Proust, and faith is awakened with the
fluttering of a stained glass window lit up by candles:

...You pray all night in the school chapel
While eternal and adorable an amethyst depth
Turns forever the blazing glory of Christ...[23]

Thus the forgotten source has been found again and its
tide expands in large waves, for the verbs in the present
tense indicate that the past is being relived, that the
scene is taking place in 1912 as it did formerly, before
1900--a simultaneity that is not a mere literary game but
is needed to translate the continuity of an apparently
successive existence. Thus a fervent, abundant prayer
rises, and it is a veritable hymn to the Christ of Calvary, a primitive Christ, man and God at the same time--
no longer the tragic tortured being of Grünewald, but
rather that of Giotto, haloed and standing out against a
blue and red background.
The litany is firmly sustained by the "it is" at the beginning of each line and unrolls one by one the glorious
titles of the crucified Christ, in a series of ascending

comparisons, from the lily to the torch of fire, from the
tree to the star. It salutes Christ as a God by insist-
ing on his eternal character: "eternal, forever, which
the thickly blowing wind never extinguishes, gallows of
eternity"("éternelle, à jamais, que n'éteint pas le vent,
toujours touffu, potence de l'éternité"). It is a praise
that magnifies a bloody reality, that of a man dying on a
cross, "pale and vermilion son of the dolorous mother"
("fils pâle et vermeil de la douloureuse mère"). It is
precisely Christian, for the God whom the poet adores
("adorable") is none other than Jesus Christ in His glorified humanity. The cross of Christ is no longer the "funereal burden" for which the thief was shamed; it is no
longer "the instrument of infamy" denounced by the putrescent magician, nor the "worst of the trees," to recall
an expression of Nietzsche. Now it is transfigured by
the heights of Apollinairian poetry, so close here to that
of Claudel.

A word from the manuscript and from the draft make the
following eulogies from the pen of the author of *The Here-*
siarch less surprising for us:

> It is the beautiful lily which in spite of every-
> thing we all cultivate
> (C'est le beau lys que malgré tout nous tous nous
> cultivons)

or else:

> ...which in spite of ourselves we all cultivate...
> (...que malgré nous nous tous nous cultivons...)

The "in spite of ourselves" and the "in spite of everything" express past reservations and even forgetfulness--
and even derision. How many doubts, repudiations, mock-
eries behind this eupheuism! Who are these "we all"?
Neither Salmon nor Fleuret, nor so many of Apollinaire's
friends; perhaps it was Billy, certainly Max Jacob who had
been converted since 1909; but above all, in our opinion,
it is Blaise Cendrars who, in his *Easter*, has just saluted
Christ on the cross with respect and emotion. However, if
Cendrars' soul is a "widow in mourning" at the foot of the
cross, Apollinaire's soul can see the divine transcendance
under the appearances of the Man of Sorrows. If the poet
of *Easter* ignores the Resurrection: "Alas! Lord, You will
no longer be here after Easter" ("Hélas! Seigneur, Vous

ne serez plus là après Pâques"), the poet of *Zone* proclaims it. If the former lingers, in spite of the title
of his poem, on the mournful night of Holy Friday, the
latter will concentrate on the glorious Ascension. In all
this first part of the poem, Christ is indeed the axis
around which everything gravitates, and the man who walked
in the street can stop for a moment, for he has met not a
vague Absolute but rather the Infinite incarnated in a
man, a man-God, a son of a human mother, a God who has
suffered but Who *is* truly God and bears a name: Christ.
The desacralization suddenly brought into the poem--after
a solemn hymn--by journalistic formulas, colloquialisms
which may seem impertinent, even sacrilegious, have been
noted:

> It is God who dies on Friday and resuscitates
> on Sunday
> It is Christ who soars to the sky better than
> the aviators
> He holds the world's altitude record
>
> Christ pupil of the eye
> Twentieth pupil of the centuries he knows how
> to go about it
> And turned into a bird this century like Jesus
> soars into the air...[24]

But the irony, if it is there, does not bear on the Person of Christ; rather we see in it a rejection of senti-
mentality, a break with the emphatic tone toward which the
poet was heading, and the transformation of Christ into
an aviator is nothing but a natural resurgence of the
original greeting to the pope who was a friend of aviation. The long development of the theme of the Ascension
thus satisfies the poet's attraction to the new invention
and his aspiration to progress as well. Moreover, the
Ascension constitutes the third wing of the Pascal mys-
tery: the death of Jesus, the Resurrection, the Ascension, and here again Apollinaire reveals himself as more
Christian than Cendrars. He recreates, in his own manner, an Ascension that is at the same time the Ascension
of Christ as narrated by St. Luke and the ascension of
the centuries, in particular of the twentieth century, in
terms of human ascension. A baroque and luxurious depiction but one interrupted with comical elements, in response

to Marinetti's wish "to kill solemnity." Alfred Jarry, in a satirical story, had told the Passion of Christ in the manner of a sportswriter and had ended his essay thus: "It is also known that he continued the race as an aviator." A willful degradation, conscious and sarcastic. How different are the words of Apollinaire, who never denied in the course of his poem his initial affirmation: "Alone in Europe you are not ancient O Christian faith"! However, it must be recognized that the depiction of the Ascension borrows from a conception exterior to religion more than from its spiritual message. In it, Christ is greeted as a miracle worker rather than as a master of life; he is escorted by aviators who are rather more like magicians, from Elijah to Simon; and "these priests who rise eternally holding up the host" ("ces prêtres qui montent éternellement élevant l'hostie") perform a process that was not asked of them. In brief, one has the impression that one strays little by little from the core of religion in order to admire nothing more than its exterior manifestations; one has the impression that it is only a superior mythology, which has gathered the most beautiful legends of the mythologies that preceded it. Would the Gospel be, then, nothing more than a great religious feuilleton, highlighted by triumphal theophanies? Would not the Christ of *Zone* then become the most Christian of idols? Let us answer this question forthwith by saying that he is also, in *Zone*, the Redeemer who, after suffering on the cross, delivers man from sin. And in this very development can one not sense a glorification of Christ as the promoter of progress according to the poet's affirmation at the beginning of his poem? The Ascension is indeed the festival of human progress and in the glorified Christ appear the premises of the glorification of humanity. Hence the joy that lifts up the lines of *Zone*, a joy comparable to the last pages of *War Pilot* *(Pilote de guerre)*,[25] which, while saluting Christianism, call for a modern Christ, whereas the Christ of *Zone* remains the Biblical Christ from the beginning of the poem to its end.

An abrupt break separates the two great parts of the poem. An allegro (the modern world, aviation, simple and new religion, the pretty street, the young street, the living Christ, the exuberant ascension) is followed by the

largo, introduced very early by the two verses that can
be described as *mezza voce*:

> And you whom the windows are watching shame is
> > holding you back
> From entering a church for confession this
> > morning...
> (Et toi que les fenêtres observent la honte
> > te retient
> D'entrer dans une église et de t'y con-
> > fesser ce matin...)

Two lines of internal feeling, showing a heavy anxiety,
announcing a confession that now rises to the poet's lips.
At the threshold of *Zone*, the greeting to the pope was
followed by an aspiration to be delivered of a sinful burden; and the first sequence, full of salutation to Christ
crucified but glorious, is opposed to the second one,
dedicated to the confession proper. Let us understand by
this a soul searching, a recapitulation of life in time
and space, a critical judgment of life, an appeal to salvation, to purification, and even, in a strange verse, to
the certitude that forgiveness is granted thanks to the
redeeming blood of Christ. Thus it is indeed in the
strong, sacramental sense that one must understand the
term "confession" as used here. Apollinaire is full of
surprises! Who would have imagined him wishfully "entering a church for confession"? Let us not neglect this
second face which he is presenting. At the same time as
a poet zesting for life, there cries in him a child searching for his soul. The man who sings of the modern city
and marvels at the poetry of the street is also the man
who suffers from solitude: "Now you are walking in
Paris all alone in the crowd" ("Maintenant tu marches
dans Paris tout seul parmi la foule"); a man who suffers
from loss of love and, even more, from loss of faith.

> If you lived in olden times you would enter a
> > monastery
> You are ashamed when you catch yourself saying
> > a prayer
> You are mocking yourself and like the fire of hell
> > your laughter is crackling...[26]

How unexpected is this first cry, this aspiration to

religious life, the unreality of which excludes all possibility of realization! Is it the result of a simple
love disillusionment? This is too easy an explanation.
The poet longs for conversion, renewal, a return to primitive innocence. It seems that he can obtain it only
through a total change of life, a definitive farewell to
mediocrity, even a renunciation of love, the shame or
even the disgust of which is expressed several times in
Zone. One is tempted to see in this extreme position a
poetic exaggeration, a sort of hyperbole that goes beyond
the deep thought; but four years later the same aspiration will be expressed again in identical terms, this time
in prose, in a letter to Madeleine dated May 7, 1916, when
Apollinaire, hardly recovered from his wound, detaches
himself from his fiancée, and seems tired of love, tired
of life—or of his life?

> I am no longer what I was from any point of view,
> and if I listened to myself, I would become a priest
> or a monk. My book, which has just come out, is so
> alien to me.[27] (TCS, p. 349)

We shall come back to this note, but do not the lines
from *Zone* reveal, similarly, a new Apollinaire, a man estranged from the tales or the free thinking works that he
had just published, in which neither churchmen nor mon-
asteries play an important role!
How can one not recall, in this regard, the repetition
of similar expressions under the pen of Saint-Exupéry?
First of all, the following lines written in 1938, which
will help to understand the despair with which the second
part of *Zone* is saturated:

> If I could have faith, I would become a Dominican.
> But one cannot become a Dominican without faith. It
> would be cheating shamefully. That's why I feel
> desperate.[28]

And five years later, Saint-Exupéry repeats again this
absurd hypothesis:

> If I had faith, it is indeed certain that, after
> going through a period of necessary and thankless
> jobs, I could bear to be only in Solesmes.[29]

In Apollinaire's lines (from *Zone*), the rime of "mon-

astère"(monastery) calls for "prière" (prayer) and the
poet repeats what he was saying at the beginning of *Zone*:
the human respect that was keeping him from entering a
church still keeps him from surrendering himself to a dialogue with God. This recalls the "poor prayers" in the
cell of the Santé, prayers so poor that they were not
published. Instead of surrendering to his élan towards
purity, the poet has cut short all emotional effusion, has
stifled with sarcasm any impulse at remorse, for it is
indeed remorse that is in question and no longer simple
human respect. But to split oneself in such a way, to
destroy the most noble part of oneself, to hate oneself
so, is this not to become one's own executioner, is this
not to feel the torments of the damned? From the re-
splendent skies where the ascension of Christ and of the
twentieth century was taking us, here we are falling back
to the deepest part of hell, from light to shadow. What
a fall!

> You are mocking yourself and like the fire of hell
>   your laughter is crackling
> The sparks of your laughter cast a glow upon the
>   depth of your life
> It is a picture hanging in a gloomy museum
> And sometimes you come to look at it closely...[30]

This fall recalls the novel of Camus and his hero who
walks the deserted streets: "Ah! my friend! do you know
what is the solitary creature wandering in the big cities!"
("Ah! mon ami! savez-vous ce qu'est la créature solitaire
errant dans les grandes villes!") Similarly, the poet
scans by means of several "you are walking"("tu marches")
("In Paris...in Paris towards Auteuil"/"dans Paris...dans
Paris vers Auteuil"/) his search for lost time--perhaps
his search for a judge or for a savior? As for the
"crackling" "laughter," it recalls the derisive laughter
that Victor Hugo describes in two lines that are akin to
those of *Zone* and express a similar drama:

> Close to the need for believing a desire
>   for denying
> And the mind that laughs derisively next to the
>   heart that cries...[31]
>   *(Songs of Twilight)*

Finally, here are the most extraordinary lines of the poem, the most extraordinary because of what they affirm and because of the verb tense, which seems to indicate a completed action--the certitude of accomplished purification as well as a remembrance of a particular grace:

> Surrounded by ardent flames Notre Dame has
> looked at me at Chartres
> The blood of Your Sacred Heart has flooded
> me in Montmartre...
> (Entourée de flammes ferventes Notre-Dame m'a
> regardé à Chartres
> Le sang de Votre Sacré-Coeur m'a inondé
> à Montmartre...)

The first line is the least surprising, for every so often one can find in Apollinaire's work an allusion to the Virgin, for whom he has kept an emotional attachment all his life. Even in a poem colored (at the very least) with skepticism, in *The Dome of Cologne*, the poet was addressing a prayer to "a statue with tender looks" ("une statue au regard tendre"), the Mother of God. He receives Mary's answer in the sanctuary of Chartres. Is it an echo of a real event, plausible since some pupils of St. Charles of Monaco had gone there for a pilgrimage? (Would the secretary of the congregation not have been chosen as one of the first?) At any rate, his friends and his teachers must have told him about this Chartres pilgrimage; he went there in thought; and why not in fact, a little before writing *Zone*? Apollinaire liked to visit churches, and even--they say--made the sign of the cross there (did he pray also?) Thus, did he never notice the black Virgin surrounded with bushes of tapers? The following is a strange remark the very year when Charles Péguy went to Chartres for a pilgrimage, when he met the eyes of Notre-Dame: "Star of the sea, Here is your glance" ("Etoile de la mer, Voici votre regard"). The same year, the same place, the same cry!

Mary is the intermediary between God and men, the Mediator, as was expressed in two lines of the draft of *Zone*:

> And even today when I am unhappy and sad
> Virgin Mary you attract toward me the divine
> glance of Christ...

> (Et encore aujourd'hui quand je suis
>   malheureux et triste
>   Vierge Marie vous attirez sur moi le
>   regard divin du Christ...)

Apollinaire follows a traditional path in Catholic
prayer and meets in a personal dialogue, for the first
and only time of his life (if one limits oneself to the
testimony of his oeuvre), Christ the Redeemer. It is a
meeting that everything was calling for, one that the
yearning for confession, at the very beginning of the
poem, demanded as a logical follow-up. The confession
made, the sin judged, one waited for absolution, one
waited for the happy words that the priest says to the
penitent: "May the Passion of our Lord Jesus Christ...
gain for you the remission of your sins," one waited for
purification by blood. We see it operating here in the
one line where the poet addresses himself to God and
applies to himself the benefice of Redemption. How far
we are from Cendrars, who honored Christ and understood
the universality of His Sacrifice, but who had with Him
no particular relationship and could forget Him without
there having been any personal contact between them! In
Zone, the absolution seems to have taken place in a real
cadre: the basilica of Montmartre which, it is very
probable, Apollinaire entered one day. His friend Max
Jacob spent nights in prayer there, and it is he, it
seems, rather than Apollinaire, who could have written
the lines of *Zone*--Jacob, who had converted, who was
falling back into sin, who went to confession in order
not to sin again, who called Christ for help. We know
of no such behavior on Apollinaire's part, but just the
same we cannot ignore these two lines, strange and yet
natural in a poem of confession, quickly forgotten, even
rubbed out by the final farewell, but lines that perhaps
contain one of his rarest secrets.

A series of short tableaux follow, in different places
where the poet is attempting to find himself. The same
obsession with sin and purification is revealed there,
in traits worthy of the most authentic Christianism:

> Now you are by the shore of the Mediterranean...
> With your friends you are taking boat rides

> One is a Nissard there is a Mentonasque and
> two Turbiasques
> We look with fear at the octopi of the deep
> And among the algae swim the fish images of
> the Savior...[32]

There again, and as in the case of the other references
to trips, the remembrance is too precisely localized--
one could cite names: Dupuy, Toussaint-Luca, Onimus?--
for it not to be in reference to a real event. But just
when one expected an explosion of happiness at the evocation of an enchanted landscape, the natural setting of
this born Mediterranean--and this contentment breaks
through in the recalling of the fragrance of lemon trees,
and in the game of the dialectal names that sing so pret-
tily--it is fear that wins over before the hideous mon-
sters, which symbolize, by their blackness and their re-
pulsive shape, the formless knot of our vices. Always
the obsession with sin and always the recourse to puri-
fication--the call to Christ the Savior. In the poem of
The Bestiary, Apollinaire found ingenuous amusement in
relating the images of the fish with that of Jesus; here,
it now provides consolation for him.

Let us skip the list of trips that the poet recalls
before arriving to the central, most explicit confession:

> You have taken painful and joyful trips
> Before noticing the falsehood and the age
> You have suffered from love at twenty and at thirty
> I have lived like a crazyman and I have
> wasted my time
> You no longer dare to look at your hands and at
> every moment I would like to sob
> About you about the one I love about everything
> which has frightened you...[33]

It is indeed a penitent who cries here; it is the confession of a poorly loved who might recognize himself
as a poor lover; it is the echo of a line from the *Great
Testament* or from *Wisdom,*[34] or from a Biblical psalm or
a modern psalm, such as the one by Claudel entitled
Shadows (Ténèbres):

I listen, and I am alone, and terror invades me...
Here again is the taste of death between my teeth...
Nothing but the night which is common and incom-
                    municable...35

Let us take these words seriously; this radical "falsehood" ("mensonge") of life, which the poet has experienced, is indeed the supreme sin--hypocrisy, that is,
the mask that has finally stuck to the skin. At moments
of distress, truth bursts out and then appears the intimate dislocation, the tearing of oneself, the divorce
between what one is and what one should be--and the atro-
cious joy at having killed the best of oneself ("You are
mocking yourself and like the fire of hell your laughter
is crackling..."). *Zone* is not a palinode but a lucid
judgment on a life, a judgment made in reference to a
faith, and therefore the poet can indeed talk of "wasted"
time and "insanity." A word in the draft, later deleted, already expressed this judgment: "the insanity of
my life and these fumes" ("les folies de ma vie et ces
fumées"). It is also necessary to consult the draft in
order to understand the mysterious "You no longer dare
to look at your hands" ("Tu n'oses plus regarder tes
mains"). Why this shame if not because these hands are
those of a criminal? Such is the first thought to come
to the mind of the reader. But the first draft pointed
to a different direction: "I no longer dare to look at
the cross" ("Je n'ose plus regarder la croix"). An authentically religious confidence, the delicate feeling
of a sinner full of humility. Until now, he had admitted his shame at saying a prayer, then at having to un-
dergo confession, now he is ashamed to raise his eyes
towards Jesus on the cross, so much does he feel guilty
and impure; as Verlaine said, "Truly I do not dare"
("Vraiment je n'ose"). And yet, during a long couplet,
the poet had celebrated the joyful cross "tree always
thick with all the prayers, six-pronged star" ("arbre
toujours touffu de toutes les prières, étoile à six
branches"). But there is in him a double movement: the
élan towards Christ and the shame of being unworthy, the
call for purification and the fear of being too far removed from it. The confidence was so precise that, either
through modesty or human respect ("You are ashamed when
you catch yourself saying a prayer"), Apollinaire has
delicately blurred it out.

He has even suppressed some lines that might have defined the origin of his orphan complex or his illegiti-
macy:

> I feel abandoned on earth since my earliest age
> I do not dare to trust myself to the star like
> the Magi...
> (Je me sens abandonné sur terre depuis mon plus
> jeune âge
> Je n'ose pas me confier à l'étoile comme les
> rois mages...)

These are precious secrets: a fatherless child, mocked
by his school chums; a son who has taken his sin from his
mother; a baptized being who could not remain faithful
to the star of his original faith: "Farewell youth
white Christmas/When life was nothing but a star" ("Adieu
jeunesse blanc Noël Quand la vie n'était qu'une étoile"),
he will later say in *The Hills*. From then on, in the
glance thrust upon emigrants and unhappy people, in the
next sequence of *Zone,* one must read more than a wholly
human compassion and recognize the desire for a treasure
that they are possessing:

> You look at these poor emigrants with eyes full
> of tears
> They believe in God they pray the women nurse
> their children
> They have faith in their star like the Magi...[36]

Where does this ample, admirable widening of perspec-
tive come from, this passing from an individual anguish
to universal misery, or more precisely to the misery of
the poor, the exiled, outlaws, Jews, destitute bums,
prostitutes? In our opinion, from Cendrars' poem, in
which the poor were those for whom Christ made his sacrifice, those who were around him on Calvary. And this
is what the draft of *Zone* indicates when it compares the
Jewish women and the holy women of Golgotha. Even if
the evangelical reference is implicit, the sequence of
Zone consecrated to the world of misery is profoundly
religious. It opens the way to the world of Charity--
with, it must be admitted, some disconcerting elements,
excessive with regard to common morality, such as the
pitiful kiss to the prostitute, which represents compassion, "immense pity," but at the same time complacency

toward sin. The latter detail is the prelude to the
abandoning of hope, to the renunciation of a possible
conversion. It is the first drought of poison: "And
you are drinking this alcohol which burns like your life"
("Et tu bois cet alcool brûlant comme ta vie"), an existence that has become bitter and feverish, fiery and
consuming: spirits of life (*eau-de-vie*), spirits of
death (*eau-de-mort*)! It is the plunge into unconscious-
ness, the desire for sleep and annihilation. The process will end in the room of the poet who will forget
this crisis by falling asleep under the shadow of fetishes: the latter will still make him think of the ob-
sessive image of Christ, under a weakened, far away, and
almost degraded form:

> You are walking towards Auteuil you want
> to go home on foot
> In order to sleep among your fetishes from
> Oceania and Guinea
> They are Christs of another form and another hope
> They are the inferior Christs of
> obscure hopes...[37]

No, Christ is not "only a fetish...born from the immense human fervor" but the "unknown god" adored by the
savages of Africa or Oceania, as St. Paul would say.
Apollinaire was one of the first to understand the sacred
character of Negro art and the fact that the fetish is
part of a religious universe; in his case, it is not mere
aesthetics. It can be explained by the fact that everything in *Zone* recalls Christ, is a reference to Christ.
He remembers his youth and he thinks of Christ. Christ
in the midst of the four elements: torch of fire, bird
of the sky, fish of the sea; and, on earth, the face of
the unhappy. Thus, is *Zone* the poet's search for Christ
or the Savior's insistent call to the sinner who is slip-
ping away?
But Christ did not triumph. The blood of Christ had
been shed in vain. The source that had been lost and
then found is here lost again forever. If *Zone* is tragic, it is because it expresses an existential anguish,
but it is also because it is an end, the end of love,
the end of faith--and the death of a God definitively
killed. *Zone* or a killing, a capital execution, suddenly decided upon, and this is what is suggested by the

last words of the poem, frightening in their unbelievable concision:

Farewell Farewell
Decapitated sun
(Adieu Adieu
Soleil cou coupé)

Even if behind this "sun" one must see a whole dying
world, the most natural explanation is to associate this
heavenly body and the Christian God, as was already
done by the poet of the *Dome of Cologne* when, remember-
ing *Easter* and its suggestive line "The sun is your face"
("Le soleil, c'est votre Face"), he spoke of the "Christ-
sun" ("Christ-soleil"). Finally, as Marie-Jeanne Durry
says so well: "we are attending the fall of a dead world,
of a slain head, of a god, and of man deprived of his
god."

Zone is not an unusual monolith standing in a work that
owes nothing to it. It is the last poem of *Alcools* and
concludes a period in the life of Guillaume Apollinaire,
but it also reveals his most intimate soul. It is at the
same time a return to youth and thus takes up again *The
Death of Pan* of his adolescence, the salute to the Christian God that rises on the corpse of the Great Pan; here,
Christ in his turn has become the Lord of the cosmos,
the Pantocreator celebrated by the Byzantine artists. In
Zone, one can see again the reopening of a wound made by
the loss of his faith, during his time at the lycée of
Nice, and which was thought to be healed. The virulent
atheism of the years after 1900 was an attempt to erase
the trace of this scar, but it only revealed it more.
And then, now and again, in a line escaping from the pen
of the poet of *The Gipsy,* of *The Song of the Poorly Loved*,
of *The Betrothal*, one could feel the sudden gasp of a
secret suffering, the longing for a dead God, or perhaps
a God still dying. The crisis at the Santé reopened the
poorly scarred wound that is bleeding in this poem but
is going to close up forever, it would seem. *Zone*, or
the liquidation of youth; *Zone*, or the healing of a remorse. It will remain for us to see, in the work of
Apollinaire that will follow, whether the farewell is
indeed definitive, if Zone will have no sequel. But this
one poem--not to be isolated from the remainder of the
oeuvre--is sufficient to reject the too hasty gen-

eralizations made about Apollinaire, to destroy superficial appearances, to reveal, behind the jovial face of
the bon vivant, a soul that has known the tragedy of existence and the torture of sin. It is not true to affirm
that there is no "escape in this poetry, no transfer
from this world toward one of faith or of longing."[38]
Zone is precisely this transfer--not an escape into imagination outside of life, but life itself in the raw.
And the realm of sacredness, if Apollinaire has indeed
found it again in the war, as was pointed out by Jean
Roudaut, he had discovered it before in the Christian
religion, which the critic defines as "bloodless." It
is not so in *Zone*, a poem more filled with sacredness
than any other, a poem nourished on the blood of Christ
--but a Christ whose blood, and this is true, completely empties in one spurt at the moment of the final decapitation:

Farewell Farewell
Decapitated sun.

4

A Godless Messianism

"There is no religious spirit in all this..."
On Prophecies

("Il n'y a pas d'esprit religieux en tout cela..."
Sur les Prophéties)

In the post-*Zone* period, from 1913 until Apollinaire's death on November 9, 1918, these momentary awakenings of a latent Catholicism disappear--or almost. God, when he is alluded to by the poet, is indeed dead; Apollinaire expresses nothing but a remote indifference toward Him. Even when he is mocking, he no longer shows the type of bitterness that presupposes an adversary who has not yet fallen. There is none of the relentlessness that emanates from *The Putrescent Magician* or *The Heresiarch and Co.* When a religious or even a Christian imagery subsists, it is an empty envelope with which the poet dresses his own conceptions, far removed from Christian doctrine unless it be completely opposed to it. Instead of God, a new idol prevails: art; instead of Catholicism, a new religion, a messianism of which the poet is a prophet as well as the messiah. As for the movements of the heart--passion, instincts--they arise from a completely pagan nature, often inimical to Christian morals: hence an explosion of sensuality, a search for overwhelming love, a hunger for an intense life of instincts

spurred on by the war, in which the dionysiac Apollinaire
revels: "the great Pan has been reborn," he then sings,
and this jovial god is himself. When, after being wounded, he reappears as a new man, and when anguish, bitterness, and discouragement are reborn, they will no longer be expressed in a poem worthy of *Zone*--with the ex-
ception of a few notations lost in the midst of an oeuvre
that is now completely estranged from religious anxiety.

Even before the war, the poems written as early as
1913 and in the course of the following year, and later
collected in *Calligrams (Calligrammes)*, are oriented to
the future; they renounce the nostalgia of song in order
to explore the present and are filled with a desire to
seize a real and concrete life through the senses. This
is shown in the first poem of *Ties (Liens)*:

...I write only in order to exalt you
O senses O beloved senses
Enemies of remembrance...

Enemies of regret
Enemies of tears
Enemies of everything I still love[1] (PW, p. 167)

One can understand that henceforth the religious allusions become rarefied. In *Calligrams*, one can count
only about twenty references to the Bible, whereas there
were ninety of them in *Alcools*. And the beginning of
the war is going to reinforce Apollinaire's desire to
live the present moment intensely, to kiss life sensu-
ally, without a shadow of remorse, without fear of sin.
What one can call Apollinaire's pagan period--according
to some of his friends it lasted all his life--reaches
its apogee at the beginning of his liaison with Lou, in
1914 and 1915, a liaison that plunges so far into eroticism that it rises up like a revendication confronting
the Christian God.

Indeed, if the religious references sometimes add a bit
of spice to a carnal passion, they show above all a rejection of all values other than physical love. Lou can
well be called a devil: "An exquisite she-devil with
bloody hair crosses herself with holy water" ("Une dia-
blesse exquise aux cheveux sanglants se signe à l'eau
bénite...") (PW, p. 426). This comparison should not

prejudge the naughty character of their caresses, for the lovers are beyond conceptions of good and evil:

> You spoke to me of vice in your letter yesterday
> Vice does not enter into sublime love
> Our love will remain as pure as a beautiful
> sky...[2] (PW, p. 398)

One senses, in spite of everything, a desire for self justification and sometimes for idealizing what the passionate lover feels to be excessive, not to say guilty, in an unleashed sensuality:

> Vice in all this is nothing but an illusion
> Which deceives only vulgar souls... (PW, p. 397)
> (Le vice en tout cela n'est qu'une illusion
> Qui ne trompe jamais que les âmes vulgaires...)

One thinks of Tartuffe! But elsewhere the poet gathers from Lou's lips "words of damnation so perverse and so tender" ("des mots de damnation si pervers et si tendres"), accepts a passion "pure or perverse,/According to what one wants to make of it" ("pure ou perverse, Selon ce qu'on voudra"), or imagines "a pure voluptuousness" ("une volupté pure"):

> And pure like the angels
> We will sing the praises
> Of your great beauty...[3] (PW, p. 437)

After Verlaine, and just as he did, the poet of *Zone* could thus whisper:

> I was a mystic and I no longer am one
> For Woman has entirely recaptured me...
> (Je fus mystique et je ne le suis plus
> Car la Femme m'a repris tout entier...)

But, contrary to Verlaine, Apollinaire does not seem to preserve "absolute respect/For the ideal which had to be renounced"("respects absolus Pour l'idéal qu'il fallut renier"). However, is this undeniable pagan completely wholesome? One can doubt it. Already, some poems reveal a deep bitterness, lassitude, and shame:

> ...I really thought I had taken all your beauty
> and I have only had your body

> The body alas does not have eternity
> The body has been given the function of enjoy-
>   ment but it does not have love
> ...I am left confused I remain disconcerted
> I feel tired of this love which you are disdaining
> I am ashamed of this love which you so despise
> The body does not exist without the soul...
> ...O you whom I possessed only as dead[4] (PW, p. 463)

This is an unequivocal confession! As was well said
by Jean Roudaut, Apollinaire got lost in his passion--
passion that could not have fulfilled his wish for eternity because its carnal nature doomed it to failure. He
writes to Lou on March 17, 1815: "You have annihilated
me during these two months" ("Tu m'as anéanti pendant
ces deux mois"). The term is true and the result of
this passion was predictable, since it was a systematic
search for defilement. Let us borrow André Rouveyre's
expression and judgment of this love affair (and Rouveyre cannot be accused of moralizing): "He surrendered
to excesses in love...They had, the daring ones, tried
to exhaust sensuality (eroticism pushed to extremes is
always accompanied morally with a very large, latent vir-
tually subconscious bitterness)." The poems addressed to
Lou, like the letters, should have remained in the private domain; we have invoked them only so as to understand a little better the remoteness from God and the
occultation of God that were implied in this passion--
or, if one prefers, in this overflowing eroticism, an
eroticism whose paganism soon acquired an unwholesome
character.

Thus the encounter with Woman was not, for Apollinaire,
a road toward God, as is so often the case for Claudel's
heroes. Lou was no more Ysé than Apollinaire was Mesa,
despite his inclinations (only poetic) towards religious
life. But another woman seems to have brought the poet
of *Zone* back, if not to God, at least to the acceptance
of a traditional Catholicism: Madeleine, the nice young
girl to whom her correspondent is trying to conform, en-
deavouring to espouse, at least in thought, her tastes
and ideals.

Can the letters to Madeleine, written for the most
part during the year 1915, be taken seriously? Let us
not forget that the soldier Kostrowitzky maintains an

amorous correspondence with several women simultaneous-
ly--that he sends to Madeleine, with slight modifica-
tions, the very poems that he is sending to Lou--poems
burning with eroticism for Lou, veiled and invoking the
future for Madeleine. And let us not forget, above all,
that his evident goal is to seduce this young girl, to
exert on her a physical spell, even by letter, wishing,
as he writes to her, that she appear in front of him
"Naked like Eve before Adam" ("nue comme Eve devant
Adam"),that she "undress soul, body, and heart" ("desha-
bille âme, corps et coeur"), and that she feel thereby
"spasms of voluptuousness" ("spasmes de volupté"). Let
us read the sophistical arguments of this pseudomor-
alist:

> To love each other without restriction is to love
> purely and thus Duty changes Hell into Paradise
> ....There is here a great poetical and ethical idea
> that is very true and that you will recall to me.
> Thus duty transforms Hell into Paradise, and the
> vices, these devils, become again what they used
> to be, that is Angels, that is Virtues. Don't for-
> get that virtues are in fact an angelical hierarchy
> and that it was Lucifer's failing in his duty that
> plunged this great light into the shadows that ob-
> scured it...[5] (TCS, p. 123)

All this deployment of the most classical angeology in
order to seduce a young girl! Apollinaire knows his
catechism, but he does not believe in it. Similarly, he
recalls the Catholic doctrine dealing with marriage according to which the priest is only a witness while the
"sacrament has the believers as its ministers" ("le sacrement a pour ministres les croyants"), but this is in
order to tell his fiancée that they are "already married"
("mariés deja"), since they desire it, and that therefore
his "wife" ("femme") must immediately surrender completely all her thoughts to her "husband" ("époux"). For
this reasoning the poet calls on the very words of Christ:
"We are now only one flesh"--a somewhat suspect interpretation! Just as his judgments on questions of religion or morality are suspect.

Madeleine writes to him that she practices her religion, and he answers: "I was forgetting to add that I

have the same religious feelings as you" ("J'oubliais
d'ajouter que j'ai les mêmes sentiments religieux que tu
as"), or again: "We resemble each other very much as
regards religion, and our ideas on marriage in church,
on the education of children are the same." ("Nous nous
ressemblons beaucoup sur ce qui concerne la religion et
nos idées sur le mariage à l'église, sur l'éducation des
enfants coïncident") (TCS, p. 113). This seems to be
very vague indeed, and it smacks of conformism, and the
following words really seem secondary: "I have on me
the medals that my mother placed around my neck when I
was a child. You can see that we are the same, my love"
("J'ai sur moi les médailles que maman m'a attachées au
cou étant enfant. Tu vois que nous sommes la même chose
mon amour") (TCS, p. 120).

The brigadier Kostrowitzky wants to insert himself into Christian civilization and thus to adopt its customs
and usages. He dreams of a proper bourgeois marriage,
and he pronounces in this regard some aphorisms that
are worthy of Joseph Prudhomme[6]: "To raise a large family is a blessing for humanity [sic]" ("élever une nom-
breuse famille est un bienfait pour l'humanité"). On
which André Rouveyre comments maliciously: "I have difficulty in believing that sacrament and law could have
succeeded in changing our clever, gracious, and deliber-
ate cajoler into the scrupulous pastor of a large family."

Apollinaire confesses to Madeleine that he does not
know Romain Rolland, and gives a fallacious reason: "the
disorders of his household had kept me away from his
books from then on" ("les désordres de son ménage m'avaient
dès lors éloigné de ses livres"). He similarly castigates
"the implacably depraved book of Laclos' *Dangerous Relations (Les Liaisons dangereuses)*, Laclos who undoubtedly invented true vice, Vice with a capital V" ("le livre
si implacablement déprave des Liaisons dangereuses de
Laclos, Laclos qui inventa sans doute le vice véritable,
Le Vice avec une majuscule"). Again, one feels like
crying out: Tartuffe!, to the editor of the oeuvres of
the Marquis de Sade, of the works kept in the reserve of
the Bibliotheque Nationale, of the pornographic novels
published sub rosa.

When he speaks of *Paradise Lost*, which his correspondent

is reading, it is to confess that he doesn't really like it, "although it is swollen with a thousand commonplaces with which our so Christian souls are still overflowing" ("bien qu'il soit gonflé de mille lieux communs dont débordent encore nos âmes tellement chrétiennes"). Which means that he no longer believes but cannot get rid of this ensemble of notions derived from religion. A Christian soul? No, but a mind cluttered with a mythology.

In the same work of Milton, Apollinaire disdains the sublime aspect about which his fiancée was speaking and develops at length the part that lends itself to sarcasm: the amorous aspect. He brings together the sublime gesture of Adam accepting the forbidden fruit from the hand of his companion, knowing that he is lost, with the gesture of the lovers who, during their embrace, transmit venereal diseases to each other. One feels that he is more comfortable in this realm than in the theological speculations of the Biblical poem.

When he quotes the New Testament, Apollinaire restricts its doctrine to the individual, and he doesn't think that Christ's precept of "love thy enemies" can be applied to nations. In this, he is following the opinion of many Christians and that of a pragmatic politician like the Cardinal Richelieu.[7] For him, Christianism, with its tendency towards universal fraternization, points dangerously to socialism.

If there are any convictions in these *Letters to Madeleine (Lettres à Madeleine)*, one can find them in the frequent appeal to a morality of Duty, a term that recurs often and is warmly and abundantly formulated, as for instance, later, in the novel *The Seated Woman*.

"I love Duty as you do and even more in a Corneille-like fashion than you" ("J'aime le Devoir comme vous et même un peu plus à la Corneille que vous"), he writes to his fiancée, and one would hesitate to take these big words seriously if they were not pronounced by an exemplary and courageous soldier who gives unreservedly of his body and strength to his adopted fatherland--who will give it his blood and his life. But the word duty does not cover, it would seem, the Christian virtues, a point that is developed in an important letter to Madeleine in which the poet speaks of her brother:

Undoubtedly, he is going to take me for a being
devoid of morality, for I have praised to him the
philosophers of life who are outside of Kantian
morality, one could almost say today Christian morality. Write to him, if you have the chance, that
the feeling of duty, for the élite, must take the
place of virtue, or that, rather, I believe that
duty creates it.[8] (TCS, p. 133)

We find again the opposition, already present in *The
Thief*, between a saddening moralism--the "humid moral
flowers" of Christianism--and an exaltation of natural
life that joins the ideal of Thélème: people who are
highly born are instinctively virtuous and do not need
any rules or restraints. Apollinaire, since youth, has
felt in his Catholicism the weight of a "funereal burden," like that of a yoke which might frustrate his tem-
perament's zest for life. He has never known that there
could be a Christian freedom through which the mind dominates time and which is expressed in the Augustinian
formula dear to Claudel and to Péguy: *Ama et fac quod
vis*!

In the era of the *sacred union*[9] and the return to the
French tradition, he takes off his hat to the old religion too insistently to be taken seriously. This can be
seen in newspaper articles collected in *Anecdotes (Anecdotiques)*. Speaking against spiritism, he approves of
practicing Catholics and even takes his place among these
good Frenchmen:

If they feel the need for piety, the French prefer
to kneel in a sanctuary, the Sacré-Coeur, Lourdes
rather than to marry religion with science in the
office of a clairvoyant...[10] (ANEC., p. 291)

But somewhat later, he defines the religious spirit as
"a mode of man's faith in himself and in his species"
("Un mode de cette foi de l'homme en lui-même et en son
espèce"). A poet before all, he enjoys the taste of popular Christmases and marvels at the legends that have
flowered with respect to the tree of earthly Paradise:

I would have a hard time to exhaust the vast literature that exists on this subject. Let it suf-
fice to say that this fantastic tree, which is the

basis for all our sacred beliefs and therefore
adorns our minds since childhood...[11] (ANEC., p.
250)

The author thinks he is speaking for the middle-class
Frenchman, Catholic by tradition, but he exaggerates his
tone: to claim that this tree is the "basis for all our
beliefs" is a manifest exaggeration. As for its value
as a myth, it is a certain one, and the old pupil of St.
Charles was right in recalling that these marvelous stories had nourished his imagination as a child: the Bible
is beautiful, but little do we care about its truth. It
is a source of the fantastic, not the source of life.

Thus, until his wound of March 17, 1916, Guillaume Apollinaire, since entering the war, lives an instinctive
paganism, a life dominated by an ardent sensuality, and
he takes from his experience as a brave soldier the conviction that honor and duty stand out as the essential
values of the war. This is what he affirms in a poem
dated December, 1915: "In honor of Honor the beauty of
Duty" ("En l'honneur de l'Honneur la beauté du Devoir").
In this respect, Jean Roudaut was able to say that for
Apollinaire the war was an especially sacred event, one
that demanded of him the practice of all virtues:

I am soon going off to war
Without chaste pity and with a severe eye
Like these warriors whom Epinal
Sold as popular Images...[12] (PW, p. 218)

An image from Epinal? Yes, rather than reality. There
is, at any rate, no reference to God, even in the midst
of most mortal dangers. And, if the soldier mentions
that he has attended mass at the front, it is only in
passing and in order to do what everyone else is doing:
an erotic letter addressed to Lou will bear the drawing
of a mass in a barn. Religion is superrerogatory, a
fact of civilization that it is proper to accept and even
to honor, but only as an exterior and social institution.

Then comes the shell fragment that wounds the poet in
the forehead. "The wound of March 17, 1916, has killed
the old man in him," says Jean Roudaut, very aptly. After
the explosion of vitality of the preceding years, we see

a relapse into bitterness and accents that sometimes recall those of *Alcools*. In particular, the phrase from a
note to Madeleine that we have already quoted in regard
to a line from *Zone*, which it reproduces almost literally:

> I am no longer what I was from any point of view,
> and if I listened to myself, I would become a priest
> or a monk. My book, which has just come out, is
> so alien to me.[13]

Is it then the former bon vivant, the sensualist, the
man not very anxious about religious matters who died on
that morning of March 17? Such indeed is the meaning of
these words, in which the poet opposes his past and the
perfect life for which he is yearning.

There is in this cry more than a simple means by which
to prepare his break with Madeleine; there is a sign of
bitterness that recalls former expressions and thus
restitutes, for a while, the climate of *Zone*. This is
confirmed by Max Jacob, in a letter to Blaise Cendrars
from the same period:

> Apollinaire is very much calmed by his sojourn at
> the front; he knows that he is an officer, and in
> this respect, he mentally remembers the priests
> who brought him up during his early childhood.[14]

Just as in *Zone*, childhood is recalled by a disgust
with the present, with the surrounding selfishness, with
works such as certain chapters of *The Poet Assassinated,*
where the "laughter" of the narrator "crackles like the
fire of Hell" ("comme le feu de l'Enfer pétille"). This
is indeed the work to which Apollinaire alludes in the
famous note to Madeleine, the book that is so alien to
him. Again we can ask ourselves: where can we find the
true Apollinaire, the deepest Apollinaire? In everyday
life or in moments of weakness? Surely he is in both.
Let us not neglect or suppress either one of these aspects.

In truth, the deepest aspect is the rarest and it soon
fades away. Just as the farewell of *Zone* was definitive,
and just as nothing similar to *Zone* will see the light
of day, so nothing will come to prolong this aspiration
to evangelical life. No religious poem, no other con-

fidence, will prove that the new man who emerged from this recent crisis is a Christian. Quite to the contrary! The discouraged man who no longer feels the beautiful ardor of the warrior needs a change of ideals, but he does not go looking for it in the religion of his youth. He seeks it in the *new spirit* defined in the poems of 1916-1918--poetic testaments, spiritual, but lacking in Christian elements except for images and references. We are thinking of *The Hills* and *The Pretty Red-Head (La Jolie rousse)*.

In the first of these poems, Apollinaire rises up before the future, at the summit of great heights, like a prophet of Israel. He adopts a peremptory tone, that of Christ, whose very words and parables he takes over:

My songs are falling like seeds...
Do not mix the tares with the wheat... (PW,p.175)
("Mes chants tombent comme des graines...
Ne mêlez pas l'ivraie au blé...")

The poet is the prophet of new times; he is Christ, he is a saint, since he recognizes that he can no longer sin:

I have finally detached myself
From all natural things
I can die but not sin...[15]

And this messiah, like the one from the New Testament, announces to men that they are called upon to become gods, after "seven years of unbelievable trials" ("sept ans d'incroyables épreuves"), comparable to the seven years of famine predicted by Joseph to the Egyptian pharaoh. "Man will become divine ("L'homme se divinisera"). Without God? Without His help? How? By a kind of sorcery, close to the discoveries of science, but without anything supernatural--through magic, not prayer. Let us learn some of these "little secrets" from the new prophet, while waiting for others "more profound." The utilization of machines and cybernetics--"order of time if the machines/Would finally begin to think" ("Ordre des temps si les machines Se prenaient enfin à penser"); psychoanalysis--"Depths of consciousness/You will be explored tomorrow" ("Profondeurs de la conscience/On vous explorera demain"); man's use of new energies: will,

kindness, acceptance of suffering--"There comes a time
for suffering/There comes a time for kindness"("Il vient
un temps pour la souffrance/Il vient un temps pour la
bonté").

These ideas of suffering and kindness, often repeated,
are new for Apollinaire, but they evidence an inclination that is more Tolstoyan than evangelical, notwith-
standing the Christian allusions: "It is the time of
ardent grace" ("C'est le temps de la grâce ardente"). It
is a metamorphosed Christianism that underlies the *new
spirit*, and rather a religious ersatz than a faith, a
magic--such is its best definition--recurring in synony-
mous terms throughout the poem: "art of predicting,"
"time of magic," "talisman," "towers," "prodigies," "secrets."

Answering *The Hills*, the poem of *The Pretty Red-Head*,
at the end of *Calligrams*, uses religious formulas with,
it would seem, an assurance tempered with humility. The
poet no longer has the audaciousness to proclaim himself
a saint, but confesses sins which are not purely literary:

> Have pity for our errors pity for
>   our sins (PW, p. 314)
> (Pitié pour nos erreurs pitié pour nos péchés)

Man is no longer god, but God guarantees the perfection
of order:

> You whose mouth is made in the image of God's
> Mouth which is order itself...
> (Vous dont la bouche est faite à l'image de
>   celle de Dieu
> Bouche qui est l'ordre même...)

Thus, once again, the poet refers to Genesis in order
to celebrate poetic creation. The period of the mocking
tone of *The Dome of Cologne* is really finished. The last
word of the poem and of *Calligrams* is a miserere: "Have
mercy on me" ("Ayez pitié de moi"). However, *The Pretty
Red-Head* trembles with a hope for eternity, incarnated in
the feminine hair of an "adorable red head"("adorable
rousse"):

> Her hair is of gold one would say
> A beautiful lightning which will last...
> (Ses cheveux sont d'or on dirait
> Un bel éclair qui durerait...)

Thus, in the "torch of red hair, which the wind does not extinguish" ("la torche aux cheveux roux que n'éteint pas le vent"),the eternal Christ of *Zone* has been replaced by a woman who exerts a quasi-divine power, a woman who is merged with the sun, a pledge of the time of "ardent Reason." Like Mesa before Ysé, Apollinaire found in Jacqueline (whom he will soon marry) the promise of flamboyant eternity, but a promise that owes nothing--in contrast with Claudel--to Divinity. It is truly a godless messianism that the spiritual testaments of the poet of *Calligrams* are preaching.

We must bid farewell to the poet, for the last works of Apollinaire are a novel, *The Seated Woman*,published after his death,and a drama in verse,*Color of Time (Couleur du temps)*written in 1918, which are hardly worthy of *Alcools* or *Calligrams*. A fair number of allusions to religious matters are scattered throughout these two works and point to a detachment that is more contemptuous than a frank attack.

More than anything else, *The Seated Woman* is a highly colored chronicle of the story of the Mormons, which Apollinaire had been researching for a lone time and which he will surround with fantastic variations covering a thousand diverse subjects, almost all of which deal with sexual questions.

The repopulation of France and the polygamy of the Mormons becomes a pretext for lusty or licentious jokes. The novelist supports his description of these immoral or libidinous practices with Biblical quotations:

> There were nothing but sermons, canticles,fulfill-
> ment of the desires of the flesh according to human
> and divine law,which demands polygamy according to
> the example of the patriarch and that of Christ,
> who had three wives, as can be seen in the Gospels
> ...[16] (SW, p. 70)

This is a blatant deformation of the sacred texts, in an imitation of Voltaire, leading to unconscious blasphemy that is amused rather than nasty. Whom is the author mocking? A ridiculous sect, or Catholicism, or any religion? He seems to be taken in by his own game when he preaches the repopulation of France and holds that polygamy would suppress prostitution and debauchery and

would allow for an increase in children. He salutes Catholic priests, who "live better than those of any other
religion" ("vivant mieux que ceux de n'importe quelle religion"), and his hero thinks that the Mormon church "is,
with respect to Catholicism, nothing but its modern continuation as adapted to new revelations" ("n'est au catholicisme que sa continuation moderne et adaptée aux nouvelles révélations"). Indeed, here is a book in which,
yet again, Apollinaire takes pleasure in depicting here-
siarchs, in stigmatizing--not without complacency--their
sensual customs, thereby degrading, it would seem, as in
The Heresiarch and Co., the mother religion, Catholicism.
Just as in the first collection of tales, the sacred texts
are parodied or given an obscene meaning, as for instance
in the following speech of the prophet of the Mormons:
"Grow and multiply, children of the Gods! Lust divinizes
us, we go up to heaven when we feel it" ("Croissez et
multipliez, enfants des Dieux! La volupté nous divinise,
nous montons au paradis quand nous la ressentons") (SW,
p. 121). Or as in this parody of the words of Christ:
"Let him who is not polygamous in Europe throw the first
stone at the Mormons!" ("Que celui qui n'est pas poly-
game en Europe jette la première pierre aux mormons!").

But we need not look, in these jests, for the author's
true position. He has himself defined it, rather clearly,
in the words of one of his characters, Anatole de Saintariste, who rejects the old religions as superstitions
and preaches a new religion, that of honor. Let us first
listen to his critics:

> The renewal of religious ideas which is noted every-
> where is misguiding. Superstitions and religious
> beliefs are so contiguous that one would have to be
> clever indeed to want to point to the exact border-
> line between one and the other, even in the bosom
> of a same religion...[17] (SW, p. 148)

Thus, such is the lesson to be derived from the story of
the Mormons, but here is the new religion preached by the
mouthpiece of the novelist:

> All Anatole de Saintariste's religious feelings had
> become transposed into the realm of social honor...
> He dreamt only of founding one religion, a religion
> of honor, a religion without dogmas and without

priests in which the most important goal would be
the moral and physical education of children...18
(SW, p. 149)

A religion, the author says a little later, that "allows [us] to suppress the fables of expiation and recom-
pense" ("permet de supprimer les fables de l'expiation et
de la récompense"). All this has been confirmed by Apollinaire in his *Letters to Madeleine*, and we must accept
it as his last conviction. It is a radical denial of
Zone, in which the anguish of sin and the longing for expiation could be felt.

The same is true for the drama *Color of Time*, a dramatic
poem with the cold and objective tone of a report, in
which the farewell to the dying gods of *Zone* is taken up
again without revealing any indication of emotion in the
poet's soul. *Color of Time* offers the spectator a gener-
alized twilight of the gods, a death of the gods that, in
contrast to *Zone*, does not produce suffering. Before
disappearing, the gods, all the gods, pass by in a degrading eclecticism, a mixture of barbarous idols and Greco-
Roman divinities and a Biblical Jahweh, even a Christ.
The evocation of the God of Abraham is technically exact,
one could say, for the poet imitates the theophany of
Ezechiel, but under his pen it is nothing more than an
image of Epinal:

And on a throne made of terraced flames
Of frightened angels and celestial beasts
Terrible and magnificent surrounded by golden wings
Luminous circles with a moving light
The jealous Jahweh whose name is frightening
Arrives fulgurating infinite to be adored...19
(PW, p. 949)

Always the cruel and unjust God whom the young poet of
twenty was denouncing in his first works! But Jesus himself is hardly better treated:

And the tragic cross from which blood is gushing
Through the flayed forehead through the five
                          divine wounds
Dominates the sun which adores it in fear...20

It is the bloody crucified Christ of *Zone*, but what a difference in this poem! The tone is impersonal, conven-

tional, frozen. It is the tone that can be used to speak
of any object that is devoid of any aura of prayer or
feeling. If Jahweh and Jesus are called God, this term
has no meaning; here they are gods without God. God has
died twice, for he no longer existed in the derisory pan-
theon unfolding in *Color Of Time*. And even these gods
are going to disappear in turn. The last line of the
drama takes up again the double farewell of *Zone*:

Farewell farewell everything must die
(Adieu adieu il faut que tout meure)

It is a statement of fact rather than a regret. Again,
faith has died, but without a cry, without convulsions,
without emotion.

Such would be Apollinaire's ultimate encounter with God,
if one did not have to think of his marriage on May 2,
1918, a union celebrated in the church of St. Thomas
Aquinas, a marriage that the poet *wanted* to be religious,
because it was natural, and during which he had the opportunity to "enter a church" and to come face to face
with the Christ of his childhood.[21]

"Christianism, our mythology," Renan used to say. Mythology is what it was above all for the poet Guillaume
Apollinaire, as it was the case for most French writers
from Chateaubriand on. A privileged mythology, rich in
dogmas, rites, personages, tales to enchant the imagination and cause the vibrations of sensibility.

Of the dogmas, the poet retains the strange names ("hy-
postasis" and "aseity," "triad" and "dulia") and the absurd logic ("Since the absolute falls the fall is a proof/
That which doubles becomes triple before having been"
["Puisque l'absolu choit la chute est une preuve/Qui double devient triple avant d'avoir été"]). Let us recall
the tales of *The Heresiarch and Co.* dealing with the ef-
fectiveness of the sacraments *ex opere operato*. Sensitive to the "pomp of the church" ("pompes de l'église"),
Apollinaire has restituted its luster; he has celebrated
the "gothic towers" of the dome of Cologne, the sanctuary
of Laghet, and so many other places of Christian worship,
to which we can add a synagogue on the banks of the Rhine.
He has unfolded colorful processions and celebrated complicated liturgies with the singing of hymns and sequences
in a profusion of extravagant costumes: cardinalian scar-

let mingles with the black and white of nuns, the home-
spun cloth of Capuchin friars with the robes of the pope.
It is because human beings participate in this pomp: personages from the past; patriarchs and heros of the Bible;
saints and Magi; prelates and monks of all types, and the
pope, Pius X, as well as the archbishop of Paris, or a
priest, friend of the author. Finally, how many marvelous stories are told by Apollinaire, taken from the Bible
or from the commentaries derived from it, from the Gold-
en Legend, or the *Acta Sanctorum!* How many miracles, up
to that of the most extraordinary of the greatest of all
miracle workers: the Ascension of Jesus! Apollinaire
cannot help loving this incarnate religion, this Roman
Catholicism, this visible and tangible religion, which
charms the eyes, the ears, and the imagination of an artist sensitive to the prestige of archaism, of the spectacular, of the marvelous. It is an aesthetic Catholicism
about which one can ask oneself whether it reveals or
hides God. Too often the sumptuous facade of an empty
temple, it is a fantasmagoria that is the fruit of an ir-
repressible need of illusion.

Often, too, the facade lets the cracks appear; the cathedral is deconsecrated or, even worse, it is given over
to the sabbath and to the orgies of political priests and
lubric monks, encumbered with the cadaver of a putrescent
God. Religious conceptions are dried up and reduced to a
skeletal state. One can still recognize Catholicism, but
it is truncated, deformed, disfigured, misunderstood--
a Catholicism that has turned negative, whose values have
been reversed, a sanctuary that has become a den of evil,
a lair of vices. The odor of sulphur was not unpleasant
to the author of *The Putrescent Magician*--a very light,
quickly disappearing odor. The diabolical figures that
cross through Apollinaire's work (from Merlin to Laquedem, from Simon Magus to the Baron of Ormesan) have neither the consistency nor the malefic power of those of
Georges Bernanos! And yet one cannot deny the attraction
to heretics, the love of profanation, the virulent anticlericalism, which reign in a good part of this work.

But another part, a restricted one it is true, one more
discreet, more profound, raises in the heart of the oeuvre,
up to *Zone* (and in *Zone* above all), a chapel filled with
divine presence. In it, Christianism is exalted; the pope

appears as a figurehead of Europe; the priests "rise eternally elevating the host," Mary lowers a tender glance towards her faithful believer; Jesus Christ, the God of youth, radiantly carries off the modern world in his Ascension. And, in the shadow of a pillar, contemplating from afar the Christ who is showing his gaping wound, a man, in whom we must indeed recognize Apollinaire, whispers a psalm of penitence.

The poet of *Alcools* is--according to an expression of M. Décaudin--"wholly contained in these apparent contradictions." Under the practical atheism there remains, at least until *Zone*, a latent Catholicism, a vague religiosity that sometimes culminates in a true faith, albeit an extremely tenuous and vulnerable faith, a childish faith. The radical atheism that follows *Zone* allows us to understand better, retrospectively, the place that religion held in Apollinaire's oeuvre--whether he fought it or exalted it. Not a primary place, for it is not religion that forms the inner unity of Apollinaire--even if one could find a unity in this man of a thousand faces. But religion has an important place, nonetheless, because it reveals his dramatic and concentrated self. We can take up again André Gide's question on the blessing or harm that the ferment of faith could have brought to his own work: "Would the absence of drama have necessarily been an impoverishing factor? Without this Christian formation, I would not have written" ("L'absence du drame eût-elle été nécessairement un appauvrissement? Sans cette formation chrétienne, je n'eusse écrit"). Let us apply this thought when we think of Guillaume Apollinaire: without the Christian formation, neither the stories of *The Putrescent Magician* and *The Heresiarch and Co.* nor the poems of *The Thief, One Evening,* and *Zone*, nor the texts that we can cite after that.

When Apollinaire died on November 9, 1918, and his friends came to visit him, several of them were struck by a contrast that seemed to them to symbolize an intimate contradiction: hanging on the wall, by the bed, a lusty engraving, and, between the joined fingers of the dead man, a crucifix--on the chest of the poet, the Christ of *Zone*, planted forever in the heart of his oeuvre.

Translator's Notes

PREFACE

1. Michel Décaudin, Introduction to Guillaume Apollinaire's *The Amorous Devils: Les Diables amoureux,Paris,* Gallimard, N.R.F., 1965.
2. According to André Fonteyne, in the work cited in the bibliography.
3. See the Bibliographical Note elsewhere in this volume.

CHAPTER I--PIOUS YOUTH (pages 5-19)

1. Chateaubriand, who wrote *Les Mémoires d'outre-tombe,* which were published after his death.
2. O Sainte Vierge
   M'aimez-vous encore
   Moi je sais bien
   Que je vous aimerai
   Jusqu'à ma mort...
3. ...Le matelot qui fut sauvé
   Pour n'avoir jamais oublié
   De dire chaque jour un Ave
   Me ressemblait me ressemblait...
4. Je me souviens des fêtes de l'Epiphanie...Ces fêtes des rois mages, pendant lesquelles je mangeais tant de

dragées fourrées d'écorce d'orange, tant de bonbons à l'anis m'ont laissé un arrière-goût délicieux...

5. ...Lorsque je ne jouais pas à la mourre, il m'arrivait de dire la messe. Une chaise devenait l'autel que je parais de petits candélabres, ciboires, ostensoirs de plomb...

6. ...Le moine était un beau garçon qui portait une couronne de cheveux noirs et drus; sa robe était tachée de vin, de graisse et marquée de petites saletés consistantes et sèches...L'opération dura une demi-heure, prenant toute l'attention de ma mère, tandis que je n'étais occupé que du cartomancien, dont la robe s'était ouverte et le montrait nu au-dessous. Il eut l'audace, lorsque les cartes furent épuisées, de se relever ainsi, bestialement impudique, et de refuser les cinquante centimes que ma mère lui offrait, en faisant semblant de ne rien voir...

7. ...Le religieux nous bénit en disant que les dents qu'il arrachait étaient le seul salaire qu'il demandât. Depuis j'ai pensé que ces dents devenaient probablement et très justement des reliques révérées.

8. A "collège" in the French sense is a private secondary school, not a university, and is usually administered by a religious order.

9. A "lycée," in contrast to the "collège," is a public secondary school.

10. C'est à la mélopée des vêpres que j'ai puisé le sens de cette prosodie empruntée aux psaumes qui exaspère tellement les tenants de notre bel alexandrin...

11. It must be noted that the progression of classes in French secondary schools is numbered in a different manner than in America. Thus one graduates from the fourth class into the third class and so forth. The first class is the most advanced one.

12. "Images d'Epinal": a popular form of illustration that became very widespread at the beginning of the nineteenth century and continued into the twentieth.

CHAPTER 2--The Death of God (pages 20-50)

1. The hero of Georges Bernanos's famous novel *Journal of a Country Priest* (*Journal d'un curé de campagne*), written in 1936.

2. "L'impureté ne détruit pas cette connaissance (de Dieu), elle en anéantit le besoin. On ne croit plus parce qu'on ne désire plus croire."

3. Couffignal undoubtedly refers to the Parnassian school of poetry, which reached its height during the second half of the nineteenth century and which was famous for its stylistic purity, precision, and objectivity.

4. One of Flaubert's tales in *Trois Contes*.

5. Les dieux narquois partout se meurent
   Et s'émeuvent les enchanteurs
   Les fleurs se fanent les fées pleurent...

6. J'adore un Christ de bois qui pâtit sur la route
   Une chèvre attachée à la croix noire broute
   A la ronde les bourgs souffrent la passion
   Du Christ dont ma latrie aime la fiction...

7. A novel written by Anatole France

8. J'ai veillé trente nuits sous les lauriers roses
   As-tu sué du sang Christ dans Gethsémani
   Crucifié réponds Dis non Moi je le nie...?

9. Vois les vases sont pleins d'humides fleurs morales
   Va-t'en mais dénudé puisque tout est à nous...
   Va-t'en errer crédule et roux avec ton ombre...

10. Michel Décaudin, Introduction to Guillaume Apollinaire, *Les Diables amoureux*, Paris, Gallimard, N.R.F., 1965.

11. Ton dernier architecte ô Dôme devint fou
    Ça prouve clairement que le bon Dieu se fout
    De ceux qui travaillent à sa plus grande gloire...

12. J'ai dit à la mère de Dieu Toi qui souris
    Mets au bord des chemins des rosiers tout fleuris
    Et les cueilleurs de roses diront des prières
    Quand les routes en mai deviendront des rosaires...

13. A painting by an anonymous fifteenth-century German painter in the museum of Cologne.

14. Je veux vivre inhumain, puissant et orgueilleux
    Puisque je fus créé à l'image de Dieu
    Mais comme un dieu je suis très soumis au destin
    Qui me laisse un regret des antiques instincts
    Et prédit dans ma race un dieu juste et certain
    Voyez de l'animal un homme vous est né
    Et le dieu qui sera en moi s'est incarné.

15. Dieu! Dieu! Il n'y a pas de Dieu! J'arracherai cet imposteur de son trône de nuages et tous fouleront aux pieds ce vieux farceur que les caricaturistes sont forcés d'orner d'une barbe blanche pour nous le rendre respectable. Dieu, c'est l'homme...

16. L'humanité n'aime que le calembour. Le Christ dit: Tu es Pierre, et sur cette pierre j'édifierai mon

église.--Vous êtes des pêcheurs de poissons, vous
deviendrez des pêcheurs d'hommes.--Farceurs! Et quelle
langue!...

17. ...Le juif avait la tête prise dans un masque de fer
peint en rouge. Ce masque simulait une figure dia-
bolique, dont les oreilles avaient, à vrai dire, la
forme des cornets qui sont les oreilles d'âne dont
on coiffe les méchants enfants.... Nulle femme n'avait
pitié du juif. Aucune n'eut l'idée d'essuyer sa face
suante sous le masque,--comme cette inconnue qui es-
suya le visage de Jésus avec le linge appelé Sainte-
Véronique. Ayant remarqué qu'un valet de cortège
menait deux gros chiens en laisse, la plèbe exigea
qu'on les pendit aux côtés du juif. Je trouvai que
c'était un double sacrilège, au point de vue de la
religion de ces gens-là, qui firent du juif une sorte
de Christ navrant, et au point de vue de l'humanité,
car je déteste les animaux, monsieur, et ne supporte
pas qu'on les traite en hommes...

18. ...Je n'espère plus le Messie, mais j'espère le Baptême. Cet espoir me donne toutes les joies possibles.
Je vis pleinement. Je m'amuse superbement. Je vole,
je tue, j'éventre des femmes, je viole des sépultures,
mais j'irai en paradis, car j'espère le Baptême et
l'on ne dira pas le *Kadisch* pour ma mort...

19. ...On savait du Saint-Esprit qu'il viola un jour une
vierge endormie. Ce stupre avait été l'opération du
Saint-Esprit, de laquelle était né Jésus...

20. ...J'ai perdu la foi et je suis convaincu que chez
aucun homme elle ne peut résister à un examen honnête.
Il n'est pas une branche de la science qui ne contredise par des faits irréfutables les soi-disant
vérités de la religion...

21. A ta place, Omer, je commettrais ce péché. Sois
héroïque, mais demande pardon à Dieu, avant et après.
Moi je t'absoudrai quand tu viendras te confesser.

22. le sexe de Noé, joliment peint; *Les Noces de Cana*
montraient un Mannekenpis pissant du vin dans les bar-
riques, tandis que la mariée, enceinte d'au moins
huit mois, présentait son ventre pareil à un baril à
quelqu'un qui écrivait dessus, au charbon: Tokaï.

23. ...De plus, des deux agents qui portèrent le cadavre
au poste, l'un avait ri, pensant avoir-affaire à un
ivrogne. Il mourut d'une rupture d'anévrisme, le
lendemain. Le second avait essuyé avec son mouchoir
la bave qui vint aux lèvres de l'agonisant, puis il

lui avait fermé les yeux. Il vient de faire un héri-
tage qui le fait riche pour le reste de sa vie...

24. ...Un dimanche de janvier, comme il (= le héros du
conte) était allé au sermon, le pasteur parla des
sages d'Orient qui vinrent visiter Jésus dans sa
crèche. Il cita le verset de l'Evangile de Saint-
Matthieu, où il n'est rien dit quant au nombre et
quant à la condition des pieux personnages qui portèrent à Jésus l'or, l'encens, la myrrhe...

25. Les jours suivants, Egon ne put s'empêcher de penser
a ces sages d'Orient, que, bien que protestant, il se
figurait, selon la légende catholique, couronnés et
au nombre de trois: Gaspard, Balthasar et Melchior...
astrologues dont la cathédrale de Cologne s'honore de
posséder les ossements...

26. An anticlerical, anarchistic paper published in the
1930s (*calotte* means skull-cap).

27. Referred to as "l'Enfer" (Hell), it is the section of
the library where erotica are preserved.

CHAPTER 3--Mourning a Dead God (pages 51-86)

1. Hélas s'en sont venus à la male heure
   Diogène le chien avec Onan
   Le grimoire est femme lascive et pleure
   De chaud désir avec toi maintenant...

2. L'amour lourd comme un ours privé
   Dansa debout quand nous voulûmes
   Et l'oiseau bleu perdit ses plumes
   Et les mendiants leur Ave...

3. Les démons du hasard selon
   Le chant du firmament nous mènent
   A sons perdus leurs violons
   Font danser notre race humaine
   Sur la descente à reculons...

4. Beaucoup de ces dieux ont péri
   C'est sur eux que pleurent les saules
   Le grand Pan l'amour Jésus-Christ
   Sont bien morts et les chats miaulent
   Dans la cour je pleure à Paris...

5. Un aigle descendit de ce ciel blanc d'archanges
      Et vous soutenez-moi
   Laisserez-vous longtemps trembler toutes ces lampes
      Priez priez pour moi...

6. Où sont ces têtes que j'avais
   Où est le Dieu de ma jeunesse
   L'amour est devenu mauvais...

7. In his commentary on *The Brasier*, note 4, p. 71 of his edition of *Alcools, Selected poems (Alcools, choix de poémes*, Larousse, 1965)

8. Un ange a exterminé pendant mon sommeil
   Les agneaux les pasteurs des tristes bergeries
   De faux centurions emportaient le vinaigre...

9. J'ai eu le courage de regarder en arrière
   Les cadavres de mes jours
   Marquent ma route et je les pleure
   Les uns pourrissent dans les églises italiennes...

10. Ce chérubin dit la louange
    Du paradis, où, près des anges,
    Nous revivrons, mes chers amis,
    Quand le bon Dieu l'aura permis.

11. Ceux qui s'exercent à la poésie ne recherchent   et
    n'aiment rien d'autre que la perfection qui est Dieu
    lui-même. Et cette divine bonté, cette suprême per-
    fection abandonneraient ceux dont la vie n'a eu pour
    but que de les découvrir et de les glorifier? Cela
    parait impossible, et, à mon sens, les poètes ont le
    droit d'espérer après leur mort le bonheur perdurable
    que procure l'entière connaissance de Dieu, c'est-à-
    dire de la sublime beauté.

12. Que ton coeur soit l'appât et le ciel, la piscine!
    Car, pécheur, quel poisson d'eau douce ou bien marine
    Egale-t-il, et par la forme et la saveur,
    Ce beau poisson divin qu'est JESUS, Mon Sauveur?

13. Un soir je descendis dans une auberge triste
    Auprès de Luxembourg
    Dans le fond de la salle il s'envolait un Christ
    Quelqu'un avait un furet
    Un autre un hérisson
    L'on jouait aux cartes
    Et toi tu m'avais oublié...

14. A cabaret where Apollinaire and his friends used to meet.

15. Je suis Croniamantal, le plus grand des poètes vi-
    vants. J'ai souvent vu Dieu face à face. J'ai sup-
    porté l'éclat divin que mes yeux humains tempéraient.
    J'ai vécu l'éternité. Mais les temps étant venus, je
    suis venu me dresser contre toi...

16. Quoted in Michel Décaudin, *Dossier d'Alcools*, Droz &
    Minard, 1960. This poem had appeared in the *Mercure
    de France* (2/15/1934):
    Je suis Guillaume Apollinaire

Dit d'un nom slave pour vrai nom
Ma vie est triste tout entière
Un écho répond toujours non
Lorsque je dis une prière...
17. This is a play on words. *Bout-en-train* means a jo-
vial companion, the life and soul of a party; *bouc*
means a billy goat. Obviously, by this expression,
Willy wanted to allude to the pagan side of the fun-
loving Apollinaire.
18. Et je viens di dire un rosaire
Avec mes doigts pour chapelet
O Vierge sainte écoutez-les
Ecoutez mes pauvres prières...
19. Je viens de recevoir des lettres
Vous ne m'abandonnez donc pas
Jésus que l'on emprisonna
Et que les douze abandonnèrent...
20. Je viens de retrouver la foi
Comme aux beaux jours de mon enfance
Seigneur agréez mes hommages
Je crois en vous je crois je crois...
21. Que je m'ennuie entre ces murs tout nus
Et peints de couleurs pâles...

...Que deviendrai-je ô Dieu qui connais ma douleur
Toi qui me l'as donnée
Prends en pitié mes yeux sans larmes ma pâleur
Le bruit de ma chaise enchaînée

Et tous ces pauvres coeurs battant dans la prison
L'Amour qui m'accompagne
Prends en pitié surtout ma débile raison
Et ce désespoir qui la gagne.
22. L'expérience m'a prouvé trop tard qu'on ne saurait
expliquer les êtres par leurs vices, mais au con-
traire par ce qu'ils ont gardé d'intact, de pur, par
ce qui reste en eux de l'enfance, si profond qu'il
faille le chercher.
23. ...Vous priez toute la nuit dans la chapelle du collège
Tandis qu'éternelle et adorable profondeur améthyste
Tourne à jamais la flamboyante gloire du Christ...
24. C'est Dieu qui meurt le vendredi et ressuscite
le dimanche
C'est le Christ qui monte au ciel mieux que les
aviateurs
Il détient le record du monde pour la hauteur

Pupille Christ de l'oeil
Vingtième pupille des siècles il sait y faire
Et changé en oiseau ce siècle comme Jésus monte
                              dans l'air...
25. A novel by Saint-Exupéry.
26. Si tu vivais dans l'ancien temps tu entrerais
                              dans un monastère
    Vous avez honte quand vous vous surprenez à
                              dire une prière
    Tu te moques de toi et comme le feu de l'Enfer
                              ton rire pétille...
27. Je ne suis plus ce que j'étais à aucun point de vue
    et si je m'écoutais je me ferais prêtre ou religieux.
    Je suis si éloigné de mon livre qui vient de paraître.
28. Quoted in André-A. Devaux, *Saint-Exupéry*, in the edi-
    tion of *Les Ecrivains devant Dieu:* "Si je pouvais· avoir
    la foi, je me ferais dominicain. Mais on ne peut pas
    se faire dominicain sans la foi. Ce serait une tricherie
    indigne. Voilà pourquoi je suis désespéré."
29. Si j'avais la foi, il est bien certain qui, passée
    cette époque de "job nécessaire et ingrat" je ne sup-
    porterais plus que Solesmes.
30. Tu te moques de toi et comme le feu de l'Enfer
                              ton rire pétille
    Les étincelles de ton rire dorent le fond de ta vie
    C'est un tableau pendu dans un sombre musée
    Et quelquefois tu vas le regarder de près...
31. ...Près du besoin de croire un désir de nier
    Et l'esprit qui ricane auprès du coeur qui pleure...
                              (*Les Chants du crépuscule*)
32. Maintenant tu es au bord de la Méditerranée...
    Avec tes amis tu te promènes en barque
    L'un est Nissard il y a un Mentonasque et deux
                              Turbiasques
    Nous regardons avec effroi les poulpes des profondeurs
    Et parmi les algues nagent les poissons images
                              du Sauveur...
33. Tu as fait de douloureux et de joyeux voyages
    Avant de t'apercevoir du mensonge et de l'âge
    Tu as souffert de l'amour à vingt et trente ans
    J'ai vécu comme un fou et j'ai perdu mon temps
    Tu n'oses plus regarder tes mains et à tous moments
                              je voudrais sangloter
    Sur toi sur celle que j'aime sur tout ce qui t'a
                              épouvanté

34. *Le Grand Testament,* one of the most famous works by
François Villon; *Sagesse,* by Verlaine.
35. Je prête l'oreille, et je suis seul, et la
terreur m'envahit...
Voici de nouveau le goût de la mort entre mes dents...
Rien que la nuit qui est commune et incommunicable...
36. Tu regardes les yeus pleins de larmes ces
pauvres émigrants
Ils croient en Dieu ils prient les femmes allaitent
des enfants...
...Ils ont foi dans leur étoile comme les
rois-mages...
37. Tu marches vers Auteuil tu veux aller chez toi à pied
Dormir parmi tes fétiches d'Océanie et de Guinée
Ils sont des Christ d'une autre forme et d'une
autre espérance
Ce sont les Christ inférieurs des
obscures espérances...
38. André Rousseaux, *Littératures du XXe siècle,* Albin Michel, 1958, VI.

CHAPTER 4--A Godless Messianism (pages 87-104)

1. ...J'écris seulement pour vous exalter
O sens ô sens chéris
Ennemis du souvenir...

Ennemis du regret
Ennemis des larmes
Ennemis de tout ce que j'aime encore
2. Tu m'as parlé de vice en ta lettre d'hier
Le vice n'entre pas dans les amours sublimes
Nos amours resteront pures comme un beau ciel...

3. Et purs comme les anges
Nous dirons les louanges
De ta grande beauté...
4. ...J'ai bien cru prendre toute ta beauté et je n'ai
eu que ton corps
Le corps hélas n'a pas l'éternité
Le corps a la fonction de jouir mais il n'a
pas l'amour
...Je reste confus je demeure confondu
Je me sens las de cet amour que tu dédaignes
Je suis honteux de cet amour que tu méprises tant

Le corps ne va pas sans l'âme...,
...O toi que je n'ai possédée que morte
5. S'aimer sans restriction, c'est s'aimer purement, et
c'est que le Devoir change l'Enfer en Paradis...il y a
là une grande idée poétique et éthique très juste que
tu me rappelleras. Le Devoir transforme donc l'Enfer
en Paradis, et les vices ces démons redeviennent ce
qu'ils furent, des Anges, c'est-à-dire les Vertus.
N'oublie pas qu'en effet les vertus sont une hiérarchie
angélique et que c'est le manquement de Lucifer à son
devoir qui plongea cette haute lumière dans les ténèbres qui l'obscurcissent...
6. A fictitious character of the latter half of the nineteenth century who symbolizes the bourgeois par excellence.
7. Louis XIII's famous prime minister
8. ...,Il va sans doute me prendre pour un être dénué de
moral (sic), car je lui vante les philosophes de la vie
et qui sont hors la morale Kantienne, on pourrait presque aujourd'hui dire chrétienne. Ecris-lui si tu as
l'occasion que le sentiment du devoir chez l'élite doit
tenir lieu de vertu ou que plutôt je crois que le devoir la crée.
9. *l'union sacrée* was the alliance of all French political
parties for the sake of national unity on the eve of
the first World War.
10. S'ils sentent un besoin de piété, les Français préfè-
rent s'agenouiller dans un sanctuaire, le Sacré-Coeur,
Lourdes, que de marier la religion avec la science dans
le cabinet d'une voyante...
11. J'aurais peine à épuiser la vaste littérature qui exi-
ste à son sujet. Qu'il suffise de dire que cet arbre
fantastique qui est à la base de toutes nos croyances
sacrées, et par conséquent orne nos esprits dès l'enfance...
12. Je vais bientôt partir en guerre
Sans pitié chaste et l'oeil sévère
Comme ces guerriers qu'Epinal

Vendait Images populaires...
13. See note 27, chapter 3
14. Apollinaire est très calmé par un séjour au front; il
sait qu'il est officier, et, à ce sujet, se rappelle
mentalement les prêtres qui ont élevé sa première enfance.

15. Je me suis enfin détaché
    De toutes choses naturelles
    Je peux mourir mais non pécher...
16. ...Ce ne furent que prédications, que cantiques, qu'accomplissements des désirs de la chair selon la loi humaine et divine qui exige la polygamie d'après l'exemple des patriarches et celui du Christ qui eut trois épouses comme on peut voir aux Evangiles...
17. Le renouveau de l'idée religieuse que l'on constate partout est trompeur. Superstitions et croyances religieuses confinent aujourd'hui à un tel point que bien malin qui voudrait marquer la limite exacte des unes et des autres et au sein même d'une seule religion...
18. Tous les sentiments religieus d'Anatole de Saintariste s'étaient transportés dans le domaine de l'honneur social...Il ne songeait plus qu'à fonder une religion, une religion d'honneur, une religion sans dogmes et sans prêtres où l'éducation morale et physique des enfants sera la grande affaire...
19. Et sur un trône fait de flammes étagées
    D'anges épouvantés et de bêtes célestes
    Terrible et magnifique entouré d'ailes d'or
    De cercles lumineux à la lueur mouvante
    Jéhovah le jaloux dont le nom épouvante
    Arrive fulgurant infini adorable...
20. Et la tragique croix d'où le sang coule à flots
    Par le front écorché par les cinq plaies divines
    Domine le soleil qui l'adore en tremblant...
21. Not only did Apollinaire then have the opportunity to "enter a church," but also to "go to confession" there, as we learn from an unpublished letter of Madame Jacqueline-Guillaume Apollinaire: "He received the sacrament of confession, however, it was without the usual ritual procedure, it happened in the sacristy in the presence of the priest, almost man to man, so to speak" ("Il a reçu le sacrement de la confession, toutefois sans le processus rituel, cela s'est passé dans la sacristie avec la présense du prêtre, presque d'homme à homme, si je puis dire").

Texts

1. THE BIRTH OF A GOD

Death of Pan (Mort de Pan): Composed, according to us, for Christmas, 1896, at the Collège Stanislas de Cannes. Given to his friend Toussaint Luca at the Lycée of Nice, at the beginning of the year 1897. Published by Toussaint Luca: *Guillaume Apollinaire, Souvenirs of a Friend (Guillaume Apollinaire, Souvenirs d'un Ami)*, 1920, reedited 1954.

Flora and the warm Phoebus were coming back to earth,
The rumbling waves were still breaking on Cythera,
And the blond Venus, adored in these parts,
In her temple listened to the singing of pious hymns.

Olympus was filling up. The Master of thunder
Was calling for all his children who came towards their
                                    father.
A strange terror was then in the skies;
The powerful immortals had become old.

But suddenly the sky sinks into space
And in an instant the divine race passes away
While a voice cries out to the confused world:

116

"Jesus will finally be born and his reign is beginning;
He is born poor in Bethlehem; his realm is immense:
Pan! the great Pan is dead and the gods are no longer!"
                                            (*Death of Pan* PW, p. 707)

Flore et le chaud Phébus revenaient sur la terre,
Toujours les flots grondants, se brisaient sur Cythère,
Et la blonde Vénus, adorée en ces lieux,
Dans son temple écoutait le chant des hymnes pieux.

L'Olympe s'emplissait. Le Maître du tonnerre
Mandait tous ses enfants qui venaient vers leur père.
Une étrange terreur était alors aux cieux;
Les puissants immortels étaient devenus vieux.

Mais tout à coup le ciel s'abîme dans l'espace,
Et la race divine en un instant trépasse,
Cependant qu'une voix crie au monde confus:

"Jésus va naître enfin et son règne commence;
Il naît pauvre à Bethléem: son royaume est immense:
Pan! le Grand Pan est mort et les dieux ne sont plus!"
                                    (*Mort de Pan,* OP, p. 707)

2. SIGN OF CONTRADICTION (Luke, II, 34)

The Thief (Le Larron): One of the oldest poems of *Alcools*
according to M. Décaudin. One can presume the date to be
1893. Published in *La Plume*, August 1-15, 1903.

CHORUS

A stutterer bearing two jets of flames on his forehead
Passed leading a people belittled because of the pride
Of eating quail and manna every day
And of having seen the sea open like an eye

The bearded drawers of water with bands
Of black and white on their hair against evils
                              and chance
Were returning from the Euphrates and the owls' eyes
Sometimes attracted the seekers of fortunes

That chattering insect O barbarous poet
Was chastely returning at the hour of his death
To the precious forest with gemmiparous birds
With toads ripened by the azure and springs of water

A triumphal procession went by to moan under the arch
                              of the rainbow
With pale laurelled figures standing in the chariots
Statues sweating jesters ewe lambs
And the raucous anguish of peahens and ganders

The widows came first beading off grapes
Before the black bishops worshipping without knowing it
With the isoceles triangle open at the morse of the copes
Pallas and they sang the hymn to the beautiful but
                              black one

The riders threw at us into the future
Alcancias full of ashes or flowers
We shall have Florentine kisses without telling
But in the garden tonight you came well-behaved
                              and thieving

Those of your sect do they worship an obscene sign
Belphegor the sun the silence or the dog
This furtive ardor of serpents loving each other

                          THE ACTOR
And the thief of the fruits cried I am a Christian

                           CHORUS
Ah! Ah! the necklaces will clink the masks will fall
Go away go away against the fire the shadow prevails
Ah! Ah! the thief on the left in the storm
Will laugh at you like whinnying horses

                           WOMAN
Fruit-thief turn towards me your lyrical eyes
Fill the hero's sack with nuts
He is nobler than the Pythagorian peacock
The dolphin the male viper or the bull

                           CHORUS
Ah! Ah! we shall shake all night the sistrums
The Ligurian voice was it then a talisman
And if you are not on the right you are sinister
Like a grey spot or a foreboding

Since the absolute falls the fall is a proof
That which doubles becomes triple before having been
We confess that pregnancies move us
Only the bellies will be able to deny aseity

Look the vases are full of humid moral flowers
Go away but naked since everything is ours

Hear the plagal cadences of the winds' choir
And take up the bow in order to kill the unicorn or
                    the gnu

The equivocal and tender shadow is the mourning of
                    your flesh
And somber it is human and then also ours
Go away the twilight shows glimmering lights
And then none of us would believe your stories

He sparkled and drew attention like a magnet
If only he had had the voice and skirts of Orpheus
And then the women at night pretending to be heifers
Would have loved him as he was loved since indeed

He was pale he was handsome as a leper king
If only he had had the voice and skirts of Orpheus
A stone caught in the liver of an old Tanagra cock
Instead of his sad reed and funereal burden

If only he had gone to live at the court of the
                    king of Edessa
Thin and magical he would have scanned the firmament
Pale and magical he would have loved poetesses
Just and magical he would have spared the demons

Go away and wander credulous and red-headed with
                    your shadow
So be it! the triad is male but you are virgin and cold
Touch is relative but sight is oblong
The only sign you have is the sign of the cross

                                   (*The Thief*, PW, pp. 93-95)

CHŒUR

Un homme bègue ayant au front deux jets de flamme
Passa menant un peuple infime pour l'orgueil
De manger chaque jour les cailles et la manne
Et d'avoir vu la mer ouverte comme un œil

Les puiseurs d'eau barbus coiffés de bandelettes
Noires et blanches contre les maux et les sorts
Revenaient de l'Euphrate et les yeux des chouettes
Attiraient quelquefois les chercheurs de trésors

Cet insecte jaseur ô poète barbare
Regagnait chastement à l'heure d'y mourir
La forêt précieuse aux oiseaux gemmipares
Aux crapauds que l'azur et les sources mûrirent

Un triomphe passait gémir sous l'arc en ciel
Avec de blèmes laurés debout dans les chars
Les statues suant les scurriles les agnelles
Et l'angoisse rauque des paonnes et des jars

Les veuves précédaient en égrenant des grappes
Les évêques noirs révérant sans le savoir
Au triangle isocèle ouvert au mors des chapes
Pallas et chantaient l'hymne à la belle mais noire

Les chevaucheurs nous jetèrent dans l'avenir
Les alcancies pleines de cendre ou bien de fleurs
Nous aurons des baisers florentins sans le dire
Mais au jardin ce soir tu vins sage et voleur

Ceux de ta secte adorent-ils un signe obscène
Belphégor le soleil le silence ou le chien
Cette furtive ardeur des serpents qui s'entr'aiment

L'ACTEUR
Et le larron des fruits cria Je suis chrétien

CHŒUR
Ah! Ah! les colliers tinteront cherront les masques
Va-t'en va-t'en contre le feu l'ombre prévaut
Ah! Ah! le larron de gauche dans la bourrasque
Rira de toi comme hennissent les chevaux

FEMME
Larron des fruits tourne vers moi tes yeux lyriques
Emplissez de noix la besace du héros
Il est plus noble que le paon pythagorique
Le dauphin la vipère mâle ou le taureau

CHŒUR
Ah! Ah! nous secouerons toute la nuit les sistres
La voix ligure était-ce donc un talisman
Et si tu n'es pas de droite tu es sinistre
Comme une tache grise ou le pressentiment

Puisque l'absolu choit la chute est une preuve
Qui double devient triple avant d'avoir été
Nous avouons que les grossesses nous émeuvent
Les ventres pourront seuls nier l'aséité

Vois les vases sont pleins d'humides fleurs morales
Va-t'en mais dénudé puisque tout est à nous
Ouïs du chœur des vents les cadences plagales
Et prends l'arc pour tuer l'unicorne ou le gnou

L'ombre équivoque et tendre est le deuil de ta chair
Et sombre elle est humaine et puis le nôtre aussi
Va-t'en le crépuscule a des lueurs légères
Et puis aucun de nous ne croirait tes récits

Il brillait et attirait comme la pantaure
Que n'avait-il la voix et les jupes d'Orphée
Et les femmes la nuit feignant d'être des taures
L'eussent aimé comme on l'aima puisqu'en effet

Il était pâle, il était beau comme un roi ladre
Que n'avaitàil la voix et les jupes d'Orphée
La pierre prise au foie d'un vieux coq de Tanagre
Au lieu du roseau triste et du funèbre faix

Que n'alla-t-il vivre à la cour du roi d'Édesse
Maigre et magique il eût scruté le firmament
Pâle et magique il eût aimé des poétesses
Juste et magique il eût épargné les démons

Va-t'en errer crédule et roux avec ton ombre
Soit! la triade est mâle et tu es vierge et froid
Le tact est relatif mais la vue est oblongue
Tu n'as de signe que le signe de la croix

(Le Larron, OP, pp. 93-95)

3. CHRISTMAS IN REVERSE

The Putrescent Magician (L'enchanteur pourrissant): sketched out at Stavelot, in Belgium, in the summer of 1899 but not published until November, 1908.

THE THREE FALSE MAGI

...Long ago we often looked at the stars, and one of them which we saw one night, discoursing in the middle of the sky, led us Magi who came from three different realms, to the same grotto, where pious shepherds had already come a few days before the first day of this era. Since then, we, as priests of the occident, would no longer know how to be guided by the star, and yet, sons of gods are still born in order to die. Tonight, it is the funereal Christmas, and we know it well, for if we have forgotten the science of the heavenly bodies, we have learned that of the shadows, in the Occident. We had been waiting, since our decapitation, for this happy night. We have come in the deep and obscure forest guided by the shadow. Now, our leaders are pale, they are empty of blood, of oriental blood and

are pale like occidental heads. We have come here guided
by the shadow.

FALSE BALTHAZAR
to the chief, livid, white like the stains of fingernails

The son of one of the smallest of the false gods
Because of love has died very old.
To guide towards him no sideration,
Only a shadow on the earth.

FALSE GASPARD
to the chief with the complexion of virgin wax

We do not bear as beautiful presents
Myrrh, gold, and incense
But salt, sulphur, and mercury
To adorn his tomb.

FALSE MELCHIOR
to the Negro chief with the complexion of elephant skin

Oaths violated by his mother!
Fall of decapitated chiefs!
False magic gods! no sideration!
Only a shadow on the earth!

Now the false Balthazar bore the mercury, the   false
Gaspard the salt, and the false Melchior the sulphur. The
shadow, instead of the star, had been an excellent guide,
for all three stopped in front of the sepulchre, laid down
their presents on the stone, meditated for an instant and
withdrew walking one behind the other...

VOICE OF THE DEAD MAGICIAN
I am dead and cold. Fairies, go away. She whom I love,
who is more learned than I am myself and who has not conceived from me, is still keeping watch on my tomb laden
with beautiful presents. Go away. My body will soon rot,
and I do not want you to be able to ever reproach me for
it. I am sad unto death and if my body were alive, it
would sweat a sweat of blood. My soul is sad unto death
because of my funerary Christmas, this dramatic night where
an unreal, reasonable, and lost form has been damned instead of me.

THE FAIRIES
Let us go elsewhere, since everything is done, in order
to meditate on unvoluntary damnation.

. . . .

...Then came a thin man with frightening eyes, who crouch-
ed and was ardently clutching a crucifix on his breast.

SAINT SIMON THE STYLITE

Without wanting to, I have founded a city. Men had gathered around my column; thus the useless city was born.
Thus, because of my pride in suffering, I am the cause of
all the sins of my sinful city. Animals, you were wrong
in dispersing. God loves those who gather and thus say
his glory. He ordered Noah to gather two pairs of all the
animals in the ark. He blessed the flock of Laban. He
gathered the dogs on the body of the impious Jezabel.
Lord, your angels have wings. Me, the cursed one with the
terrible miracles, I was perched on a high column like a
bird and while making miracles, I was assailed by temptations, varying with the temperature. Ardabure shot arrows
at me like at a bird.

THE MAGICIAN

You abandoned the cities and the earth which supports
the cities. Higher than the earth, you were mistaken by
the proximity of the birds. But the first ones to die are
only good for predictions. Their flights are prophetic
and cursed. Let no one imitate the winged being, the first
to die. Whereof do you speak of angelic wings? I am not
winged and yet I am an angel, except for the baptism. You
yourself, you are an angel, except for the baptism, O Miraculous one!

SAINT SIMON THE STYLITE

Remember your baptism for a long time...
(*The Putrescent Magician*, Gallimard, 1921, pp.
31ff. and pp. 45ff; OC, pp. 68–70; p. 76; p. 85).

LES TROIS FAUX ROIS MAGES

...Autrefois nous regardions souvent les étoiles, et
l'une que nous vîmes une nuit, discourant au milieu du
ciel, nous mena, mages venus de trois royaumes différents,
vers la même grotte, où de pieux bergers étaient déjà venus
peu de jours avent le premier jour de cette ère. Depuis
lors, prêtres d'occident nous ne saurions plus nous laisser guider par l'étoile et pourtant des fils de dieux naissent encore pour mourir. Cette nuit, c'est la Noël funéraire et nous le savons bien, car si nous avons oublié la
science des astres, nous avons appris celle de l'ombre, en
Occident. Nous attendions depuis notre décollation cette

nuit bienheureuse. Nous sommes venus dans la forêt pro-
fonde et obscure guidés par l'ombre. Or, nos chefs sont
pâles, ils sont vides de sang, du sang oriental, et pâles
comme des têtes occidentales. Nous sommes venus ici guidés
par l'ombre.

FAUX BALTHAZAR
au chef livide, blanc comme les taches des ongles

Le fils d'un des plus petits faux dieux
Par amour est mort très vieux.
Pour guider vers lui pas de sidère,
Rien qu'une ombre sur la terre.

FAUX GASPARD
au chef couleur de cire vierge

Nous ne portons pas pour beaux présents
La myrrhe, l'or et l'encens
Mais le sel, le souffre et le mercure
Pour orner sa sépulture.

FAUX MELCHIOR
au chef nègre couleur de peau d'éléphant

Serments par sa mère violés!
Chute des chefs décollés!
Faux dieux magiques! pas de sidère!
Rien qu'une ombre sur la terre!

Or le faux Balthazar portrait le mercure, le faux Gaspard portait le sel et le faux Melchior portait le soufre.
L'ombre, au lieu de l'étoile, avait été un guide excellent, car tous les trois s'arrêtèrent devant le sépulcre,
déposèrent leurs présents sur la pierre, méditèrent un
instant et se retirèrent, marchant l'un derrière l'autre...

VOIX DE L'ENCHANTEUR MORT
Je suis mort et froid. Fées, allez-vous-en; celle que
j'aime, qui est plus savante que moi-même et qui n'a point
conçu de moi, veille encore sur ma tombe chargée de beaux
présents. Allez-vous-en. Mon cadavre pourrira bientôt et
je ne veux pas que vous puissiez jamais me le reprocher.
Je suis triste jusqu'à la mort et se mon corps était vivant il suerait une sueur de sang. Mon âme est triste
jusqu'à la mort à cause de ma Noël funéraire, cette nuit
dramatique où une forme irréelle, raisonnable et perdue a
été damnée à ma place.

Allons ailleurs, puisque tout est accompli, méditer sur la damnation involontaire.

. . . .

...Ensuite vint un homme maigre, aux yeus effrayants, qui s'accroupit et serrait ardemment un crucifix sur sa poitrine.

SAINT-SIMÉON STYLITE

Involontairement, j'ai fondé une ville. Les hommes s'étaient réunis autour de ma colonne; c'est ainsi que naquit la ville inutile. Ainsi par mon orgueil de souffrir, je suis cause de tous les péchés de ma ville pécheresse. Animaux, vous avez mal fait de vous disperser. Dieu aime ceux qui se réunissent et disent ainsi sa gloire. Il enjoignit à Noé de réunir dans l'arche deux couples de tous les animaux. Il bénit les troupeaus de Laban. Il réunit les chiens sur le corps de l'impie Jézabel. Seigneur, tu n'as fait mourir que des êtres ailes, ceux que tu préfères. Seigneur, tes anges ont des ailes. Moi, le maudit aux terribles miracles, j'étais perché sur une haute colonne comme un oiseau, et accomplissant des miracles, j'étais assailli de tentations selon la temperature. Ardabure tira des flèches sur moi comme un oiseau.

L'ENCHANTEUR

Tu délaissas les villes et la terre qui supporte les villes. Plus haut que la terre, tu fus trompé par le voissinage des oisseaux; or, ces premiers mourants ne sont bons qu'à prédire. Leurs vols sont annonciateurs et maudits. Que nul n'imite l'être ailé, premier mourant. Que parles-tu des ailes angéliques? Je ne suis point ailé et pourtant je suis an ange, sauf le baptême. Toi-même, tu es un ange, sauf le baptême, O Miraculeux!

SAINT-SIMÉON STYLITE

Souviens-toi longtemps encore de ton baptême...
(*L'Enchanteur pourrissant,* Gallimard, 1921, pp. 31 sq. et pp. 45 sq.; OC, pp.68-70; p. 76; p.85)

4. CURSED RACE, CHOSEN RACE

The Synagogue (La Synagogue): An observed scene probably composed after "Sukkot," the Feast of the Tabernacles, in 1901 (September 28) at Unkel, a town on the shores of the Rhine. Published in the *Festin d'Esope* (January, 1904).

Ottomar Scholem and Abraham Loeweren
Green felts on their heads the morning of the Sabbath
Are going to the synagogue along the Rhine
And the hills and vignards over there are reddening

They are quarreling and cry out things that one
                              hardly dares to translate
Bastard conceived during menses or Let the devil enter
                              into your father
The old Rhine raises its streaming face and turns
                              away to smile
Ottomar Scholen and Abraham Loeweren are angry

Because during the sabbath one must not smoke
While the Christians go by with lit cigars
And because Ottomar and Abraham both love
The ewe-eyed Lia with the slightly protruding belly

However in a little while in the synagogue one after
                              the other
They will kiss the torah raising their beautiful hats
Among the wooded branches of the feast of the tabernacles
The singing Ottomar will smile at Abraham

They will sing poorly without rhythm and the grave voices
                              of the men
Will make a Leviathan moan at the bottom of the Rhine
                              like a voice of autumn
And in the synagogue full of hats they will shake the
                              loulabim
Hanoten ne Kamoth bagoim tholahoth baleoumim
                              (*The Synagogue*, PW, p. 113)

Ottomar Scholem et Abraham Loeweren
Coiffés de feutres verts le matin du sabbat
Vont à la synagogue en longeant le Rhin
Et les coteaux où les vignes rougissent là-bas

Ils se disputent et crient des choses qu'on ose à
                              peine traduire
Bâtard conçu pendant les règles ou Que le diable entre
                              dans ton père
Le vieux Rhin soulève sa face ruisselante et se détourne
                              pour sourire
Ottomar Scholem et Abraham Loeweren sont en colère

Parce que pendant le sabbat on ne doit pas fumer
Tandis que les chrétiens passent avec des cigares allumés

Et parce qu'Ottomar et Abraham aiment tous deux
Lia aux yeux de brebis et dont le ventre avance un peu

Pourtant tout à l'heure dans la synagogue l'un après
                              l'autre
Ils baiseront la thora en soulevant leur beau chapeau
Parmi les feuillards de la fête des cabanes
Ottomar en chantant sourira à Abraham

Ils déchanteront sans mesure et les voix graves
                              des hommes
Feront gémir un Léviathan au fond du Rhin comme une
                              voix d'automne
Et dans la synagogue pleine de chapeaux on agitera
                              les loubabim
Hanoten ne Kamoth bagoim tholahoth baleoumim
                    (*La Synagogue*, OP, p. 113)

5. "WHEN THE CARNAL AND SACRILEGIOUS CARNIVAL RETURNS..."

The Dome of Cologne (Le Dôme de Cologne): dated Cologne,
February, 1902. Apollinaire had attended the Carnival
there. Published in the *Guetteur mélancolique,* 1952.

Your last architect O Dome became insane
This clearly proves that the good Lord doesn't give a damn
About those who are working for his greatest glory
This is what I know O Dome of your story
Hiram is a witness it is a foolish plan to build for God

You raise your two gothic towers in the middle
Of a modern square with gilded signs
Yet through your stained glass windows at every sunset
                              you bleed
Up to the Rhine drunk with gold and in the frequent wind
The blood of the Christ-sun and of the good pelican

But be modern and let your deified priests
Stretch telegraphic wires between your towers
And then you will become a lute and the storm
Will make the wires moan with an extravagant hymn

Dome marvel among the marvels of the world
The Eiffel tower and Rosamunda's palace
The black and white stork all summer
On your towers immitate your immobility

You are hiding the decay of the Magi
Your breath is incense your sighs are clouds
O Dome I am not the only one to love you

The angels each winter come to shed feathers
On your towers and the feathers melt like snow
When the carnal and sacrilegious Carnival returns

The horses of the wagons shinny in crescendo
Primo toward your hundred gargoyles and secundo
Toward you wooden horses of Richmodis-Ado

In a filled stoup Kobbes dunks his face
Next to a white cuirassier who pinches unashamedly
The buttocks of a young lady from Cologne

Funkes no longer knitting since they are tipsy
Believe they are the husbands of the eleven
                                   thousand virgins
And the beadles are afraid of their flowered guns

The deeply moved Bestevater confesses to the three Magi
That his wife has breasts as soft as cheeses
And that another Gertrude is accepting his attentions

Marizibill who sings in a soft flat German
Chooses you for a rendezvous with her fat lover
Beardless and red-headed Drikkes who is burping madly

And Venetia tired of her neuroses
Will come to offer tomorrow the Monday of the roses
Her menstrual linen soiled with hematidroses

O Dome O the auferant which the sky has robed in a cope
Of azure lined with ermine O big tufted horse
With crosses whose virtues are those of the Pentacle
                Kick whinny snort

My hard formal dreams will know how to ride you
My fate with the golden chariot will be your
                                   beautiful steeple
Which for bridles will take the ropes of your bells
                Ringing in demisemiquavers

But the Dome is the church of a marvelous god
Created by man for man has created the gods
As Hermes Trismegistus says in his Pimander
And turning to a statue with tender looks
I have told the mother of God You who are smiling
Place flowering rose bushes by the roadside
And the rose gatherers will say prayers
When the roads in May will become rosaries
                    (*The Dome of Cologne,* PW, p. 538)

Ton dernier architecte ô Dôme devint fou
Ça prouve clairement que le bon Dieu se fout
De ceux qui travaillent à sa plus grande gloire
Voilà ce que je sais Dôme de ton histoire
Témoin Hiram c'est sot calcul bâtir pour Dieu

Tu dresses tes deux tours gothiques au milieu
D'une place moderne aux dorures d'enseignes
Pourtant par tes vitraux chaque couchant tu saignes
Jusqu'au Rhin ivre d'or et sous le vent fréquent
Le sang du Christ-soleil et du bon pélican

Mais sois moderne et que tes prêtres déifiques
Tendent entre tes tours des fils télégraphiques
Et tu deviendras luth alors et l'ouragan
Fera gémir aux fils un hymne extravagant

Dôme merveille entre les merveilles du monde
La tour Eiffel et le Palais de Rosemonde
Les cigognes noires et blanches tout l'été
Imitent sur tes tours ton immobilité

Tu recèles la pourriture des rois mages
Tes respirs sont d'encens tes soupirs de nuages
O Dôme je ne suis pas le seul à t'aimer

Les anges chaque hiver viennent se déplumer
Sur tes tours et les plumes fondent comme neige
Quand revient Carnaval charnel et sacrilège

Les chevaux des chars hennissent en crescendo
Primo vers tes cent gargouilles et secundo
Vers tes chevaux en bois de Richmodis-Ado

Dans un bénitier plein Kobbes trempe sa trogne
Près d'un cuirassier blanc qui pince sans vergogne
Les fesses d'une demoiselle de Cologne

Des funkes ne tricotant plus car ils sont gris
Des onze mille vierges se croient les maris
Et les bedeaux ont peur de leurs fusils fleuris

Le Bestevater ému confesse aux trois rois mages
Que sa femme a des seins mous comme des fromages
Et qu'une autre Gertrude accepte ses hommages

Marizibill qui chante en doux plat allemand
T'élit pour rendez-vous avec son gros amant
Drikkes imberbe et roux qui rote éperdument

Et la Venetia lasse de ses névroses
Vindra vouer à Dieu demain lundi des roses
Ses linges menstruels tachés d'hématidroses

O Dôme ô l'auférant que le ciel a chapé
D'azur fourré d'hermine ô grand cheval houppé
De croix dont les vertus sont celles du pentacle
          Regimbe hennis renacle

Mes durs rêves formels sauront te chevaucher
Mon destin au char d'or sera ton beau cocher
Qui pour brides prendra les cordes de tes clothes
          Sonnant à triple croches

Mais le Dôme est l'église d'un dieu merveilleux
Créé par l'homme car l'homme a créé les dieux
Comme dit Hermès Trismégiste en son Pimandre
Et tourné vers une statue au regard tendre
J'ai dit à la mère de Dieu Toi qui souris
Mets au bord des chemins des rosiers tout fleuris
Et les cueilleurs de roses diront des prières
Quand les routes en mai deviendront des rosaires
          (*Le Dôme de Dologne,* OP, p. 538)

6. "A FAITH THAT IS AT FIRST VACILLATING HAS COLLAPSED FOREVER..."

Infallibility (L'Infaillibilité): composed, according to
us, in the summer of 1906; cf. our article in the *Revue
des Lettres Modernes,* "Apollinaire" (1965). It was included in *The Heresiarch and Co.,* published in October,
1910.

On June 25, 1906, Cardinal Porporelli was finishing his
dinner when the visit of a French priest, Abbot Delhonneau,
was announced. It was three o'clock in the afternoon. The
implacable sun which exalted the triumphant cunning of the
ancient Romans and which warms with difficulty the cold
trickery of the Romans of our time, even when it lets its
unbearable rays fall on the Piazza di Spagna where the Cardinal's palace is situated, was respectful of the apart-
ment of Mgr. Porporelli. The shades created a pleasant atmosphere of freshness and an almost voluptuous half-light.
    Abbot Delhonneau was led into the dining room. He was
a priest from the Morvon region. His stubborn appearance
was not without similarity to that of Redskins.
    He came from Autun, and he should have been born within
the Celtic walls of the ancient city of Bibracte, on Mount
Beuvray. There still live in Autun--a city of Gallo-Roman
origins--and in its surroundings some Gauls in whose veins
flows no Latin blood, and Abbot Delhonneau was one of them.

He approached the prince of the church and kissed his ring, as was customary. Refusing the basket of fruits from Sicily proffered by Mgr. Porporelli, he came to the point of his visit.

"I wish," he said, "to have a meeting with our Holy Father the Pope, but in a private audience."

"A secret government mission?" asked the cardinal, winking.

"Not at all, Monsignor," answered Abbot Delhonneau, "the reasons which make me solicit this audience are of interest not only to the Church of France, but to all Catholics."

"Dio mio!" exclaimed the cardinal, biting into a dried fig stuffed with a nut and anise. "Is it really so serious?"

"Very serious, Monsignor," repeated the French priest, while trying to scrape off the few candle drippings he had noticed on his cassock.

The prelate moaned.

"What else can be the matter? We already have enough trouble with your law on separation, and the ravings of Canon Bierbaum, from Landshut in Bavaria, who does not stop writing against infallibility..."

"Imprudent man," interrupted Abbot Delhonneau.

Mgr. Poroporelli bit his lips. In his youth, when he was nothing but a mundane Florentine priest, he had fought infallibility, but later he had bowed before the dogma.

"You'll have an audience tomorrow, Signor Abbot," he said. "You know the ritual?"

He extended his hand. The priest bowed, kissed it sonorously and withdrew while the cardinal with a weary look blessed him with his right hand, while he squeezed the peaches in the basket with the left.

When, the next day, Abbot Delhonneau was brought in to the papal chambers, he fell on his knees and kissed the mule of the white pontiff. Then, rising deliberately, he asked him in Latin to hear him out alone, as though during confession. What an act of condescension! The Holy Father accepted this daring request.

When they were alone, Abbot Delhonneau started to speak slowly. He was trying to pronounce Latin in the Italian manner, but gallicisms abounded in his seminarian speech; moreover, the French "u" was often repeated, which was incomprehensible for the pope, who interrupted the abbot and asked him to repeat what he did not understand.

"Holy Father," said Abbot Delhonneau, "after much study and painful reflection, I have acquired the certitude that our dogmas are not of divine origin. I have lost my faith, and I am convinced that it cannot stand up to an honest examination by any man. There is no branch of science that does not contradict the so-called truths of religion by irrefutable facts. Alas, Holy Father, what sorrow it is for a priest to discover these errors and what suffering to dare to confess them!"

"My child," said the pope, "I hope that under these conditions, you have stopped celebrating Holy Mass. No priest can boast of not having known the doubts which have beset you; but a retreat in this city, the cradle of Catholicism, will give you back your lost faith, and by means of..."

"No! No! Holy Father. I have done everything possible in order to recover a faith which, at first vacillating, has collapsed forever. I have tried to turn away from the thoughts which were torturing me. It was in vain! And you yourself, Holy Father, you have said it, you have had doubts. What am I saying? Doubts? No! But knowledge! Illumination! Certitude! Admit it, the triple crown which weighs on your forehead is heavy with sacred falsehoods. And even if politics prevent you from revealing the negative thoughts which dwell in your brain, they exist just the same. The fear of ruling by means of time-honored lies, that is the true burden of papacy, a burden which makes the elect hesitate upon emerging from the Conclave...

"Answer me, Holy Father: you know all this. A Roman pontiff cannot be less shrewd than a poor priest from the Morvan!"

The pope was seated immobile, grave, and during the last part of this speech, he did not open his mouth. In front of him, Abbot Delhonneau seemed to be like one of the Gauls who, during the sack of Rome, came to annoy the majestic senators who looked like statues in their curule chairs. Slowly, raising his eyes, the pontiff asked:

"Priest! What are you leading up to?"

"Holy Father," answered Abbot Delhonneau, "you wield a formidable power, you have the right to decree good and evil. Your infallibility, this incontestable dogma, because it rests upon an earthly reality gives you a rule which does not allow contradiction. You can impose truth or error upon all Catholics, by choice. Be kind! Be human! Teach what is true! Order ex cathedra that Catholicism be dissolved! Announce that its practices are super-

stitions! Say that the glorious and millenary role of the
church is over! Erect these truths into dogma and you will
have acquired the gratitude of mankind. You will then
descend with dignity from a throne where you were ruling
by error and that no one will ever be able to occupy legi-
timately, if you were to declare it vacant forever!

The pope had risen. Disdainful of any ceremony, he left
the room without saying a word to the French priest, who
was scornfully smiling and whom a guard came to lead through
the sumptuous galleries up to the door.

Some time later, the Roman Curia created a new diocese
in Fontainebleau and named Abbot Delhonneau as its head.

During his first trip ad limina, this bishop proposed to
the Holy See the creation into dogma of the belief in the
divine mission of France. When Cardinal Porporelli learned
of this, he exclaimed:

"Pure gallicanism! But the Gallo-roman administration,
what a benefit for Gaul! It is necessary to tame the turbulence of the French. And what trouble to civilize them!"

("Infallibility," in *The Heresiarch and Co.,*
pp. 70ff; OC, pp. 136-39)

Le 25 juin 1906, le cardinal Porporelli achevait de
dîner lorsqu'on lui annonça la visite d'un prêtre français,
l'abbé Delhonneau. Il était trois heures de l'après-midi.
L'implacable soleil qui exalta la ruse triomphatrice des
anciens Romains et qui échauffe avec peine la froide rouerie
de ceux de nos temps, s'il laissait tomber des rayons in-
soutenables sur la place d'Espagne où s'élève le palais
cardinalice, respectait l'appartement de Mgr Porporelli.
Des persiennes entretenaient une fraîcheur agréable et un
demi-jour presque voluptueux.

L'abbé Delhonneau fut introduit dans la salle à manger.
C'était un prêtre morvandiau. Son aspect têtu n'allait
point sans analogie avec celui des Peaux-Rouges.

Autunois, il aurait dû naître dans l'enceinte celtique de
l'ancienne Bibracte, sur le mont Beuvray. Il y a encore
à Autun, ville d'origine gallo-romaine, et aux environs,
des Gaulois dans les veines desquels il ne coule point de
sang latin, et l'abbé Delhonneau était de ce nombre.

Il s'approcha du prince de l'Église et lui baisa l'anneau
selon l'usage. Refusant les fruits de Sicile que Mgr Porporelli lui offrait dans une corbeille, il exposa le but
de sa démarche.

- Je souhaite, dit-il, avoir une entrevue avec notre

Saint-Père le Pape, mais en audience privée.
- Mission secrète gouvernementale? demanda le cardinal
en clignant de l'oeil.
- Non point,Monseigneur! répondit l'abbé Delhonneau,les
raisons qui me font solliciter cette audience n'intéressent
pas seulement l'Église de France, mais la Catholicité tout
entière.
- Dio mio! s'écria le cardinal en mordant dans une figue
sèche, farcie avec une noisette et de l'anis. Est-ce réel-
lement si grave?
- Très grave, Monseigneur, répéta le prêtre français,
tandis qu'apercevant quelques taches de bougie sur sa sou-
tane, il s'efforçait de les gratter.
Le prélat gémit:
- Que peut-il encore y avoir? Nous avons déjà assez
d'ennuis avec votre loi sur la séparation et les divaga-
tions de ce chanoine Bierbaum, de Landshut, en Bavière, qui
ne cesse d'écrire contre l'infaillibilité...
- L'imprudent! interrompit l'abbé Delhonneau.
Mgr Porporelli se mordit les lèvres. Dans sa jeunesse,
alors qu'il n'était qu'un prêtre mondain de Florence, il
avait combattu l'Infaillibilité, mais il s'était incliné
ensuite devant le dogme.
- Vous aurez audience demain, signor abbé, dit-il, vous
connaissez le cérémonial?
Il tendit la main; le prêtre s'inclina, y appliqua un
baiser sonore, et se retira, marchant à reculons jusqu'à
la porte où il s'inclina une seconde fois, tandis que le
cardinal, d'un air las, le bénissait de la main droite,
pendant que de la gauche il tâtait des pêches dans la corbeille.

Lorsque le lendemain l'abbé Delhonneau fut introduit chez
le pape, il se jeta à genoux et baisa la mule du blanc pontife, puis s'étant relevé délibérément, il le pria en latin
de l'entendre seul,comme en confession. Et quelle condes-
cendance! Le Saint-Père accueillit cette requête osée.
Lorsqu'ils furent seuls, l'abbé Delhonneau se mit à parler lentement. Il s'efforçait de prononcer le latin à
l'italienne, mais les gallicismes abondaient dans son lan-
gage de séminaire; de plus, l'u français y revenait souvent,incompréhensible pour le pape qui interrompait l'ora-
teur et se faisait répéter ce qu'il ne comprenait point.
- Saint-Père,disait l'abbé Delhonneau,à la suite d'études
et de réflexions pénibles,j'ai acquis la certitude que nos
dogmes ne sont pas d'origine divine. J'ai perdu la foi et

je suis convaincu que chez aucun homme elle ne peut résister
à un examen honnête. Il n'est pas une branche de la
science qui ne contredise par des faits irréfutables les
soi-disant vérités de la religion. Hélas, Saint-Père,
quelle peine pour un prêtre de découvrir ces erreurs et
quelle douleur d'oser les avouer!

— Mon enfant, dit le pape, je pense que dans ces conditions vous avez cessé de célébrer la Sainte-Messe. Les
doutes qui sont venus vous assaillir, aucun prêtre ne peut
se vanter de ne pas les avoir connus; mais une retraite dans
cette ville, berceau du catholicisme, vous rendra la foi
perdue, et par les mérites de...

— Non! Non! Saint-Père. J'ai fait tout ce qui était
possible pour recouvrer une foi qui, d'abord vacillante,
s'est effondrée à jamais. Je me suis efforcé de me dé-
tourner de pensées qui me torturaient. C'était en vain!
... Et vous-même, Saint-Père, vous l'avez déclaré, les
doutes vous sont venus. Que dis-je? des doutes? Non!
mais des clartés, des illuminations, des certitudes! Avouez-
le, le trirègne qui pèse sur votre front est lourd de faus-
setés sacrées. Et si la politique vous empêche d'affirmer
les négations qui roulent dans votre cerveau, elles n'en
existent pas moins. Et l'effroi de régner au moyen de men-
songes séculaires, voilà le vrai fardeau de la papauté, fardeau qui fait hésiter les élus au sortir du conclave...
... Répondez-moi, Saint-Père: Vous savez tout cela. Un
pontife romain ne doit pas être moins perspicace qu'un
pauvre prêtre du Morvan!

Le pape était assis immobile, grave, et pendant cette
dernière partie du discours il n'ouvrit pas la bouche. Devant lui, l'abbé Delhonneau semblait un de ces Gaulois qui
pendant le sac de Rome venaient agacer les sénateurs majestueux, pareils à des statues, sur leur chaise curule. Levant lentement les yeux, le pontife demanda:

— Prêtre! Où voulez-vous en venir?

— Saint-Père, répondit l'abbé Delhonneau, vous détenez
une puissance formidable, vous avez le droit de décréter
le Bien et le Mal. Votre infaillibilité, ce dogme incontestable parce qu'il repose sur une réalité terrestre,
vous donne un magistère qui ne souffre point de contradiction. Vous pouvez imposer aux catholiques la vérité ou
l'erreur, à votre choix. Soyez bon! Soyez humain! Ensei-
gnez ce qui est vrai! Ordonnez ex cathedra que le catholicisme soit dissous! Proclamez que ses pratiques sont
superstitieuses! Annoncez que le rôle glorieux et mil-

lénaire de l'Église est terminé! Érigez ces vérités en dogme et vous aurez acquis la reconnaissance de l'Humanité. Vous descendrez ensuite dignement d'un trône d'où vous dominiez par l'erreur et que nul ne pourrait désormais légitimement occuper si vous le déclariez vacant à jamais! Le pape s'était levé. Dédaigneux de tout cérémonial, il sortit de la pièce sans adresser un mot au prêtre français qui souriait avec mépris, et qu'un garde-noble, vint guider à travers les galeries somptueuses du Vatican, jusqu'à la sortie.

Quelque temps après, la curie romaine créa un nouvel évêche à Fontainebleau et y nomma l'abbé Delhonneau.

Lors de son premier voyage ad limina, cet évêque ayant proposé au Saint-Siège l'érection en dogme de la croyance à la mission divine de la France, le cardinal Porporelli, quand il l'apprit, s'écria:

-Pur gallicanisme! Mais l'administration gallo-romaine, quel bienfait pour les Gaules! Elle est nécessaire pour dompter la turbulence des Français. Et que de peine pour les civiliser!...

                    ("L'Infaillibilité," dans *l'Hérésiarque et Cie*,
                                        pp. 70 sq.; OC, pp. 136-39)

7. A PASSION IN REVERSE...

One Evening (Un Soir): Probably dates from 1904, according to M. Décaudin. Published in *Alcools*.

An eagle descended from this sky white with archangels
    And you sustain me
Will you let all these lamps tremble for long
    Pray pray for me

The city is metallic and it is the only star
    Drowned in your blue eyes
When the trams rolled by pale sparks flew
    Onto mangy birds

And all that trembled in the eyes of my dreams
    Which a single man was drinking
Under the gaslight as russet as the poisonous
                                        orange agaric
    O clothed one your arm was coiling

See the actor sticks out his tongue at his atten-
                                        tive public
    A phantom has committed suicide

The apostle is hanging from the fig tree and
                           slowly salivates
       Let us then play for this love with dice

Bells clearly ringing were announcing your birth
                  See
The roads are full of flowers and the palms are advancing
                 Toward you

                                      (One Evening, PW, p. 126*)*

Un aigle descendit de ce ciel blanc d'archanges
     Et vous soutenez-moi
Laisserez-vous trembler longtemps toutes ces lampes
     Priez priez pour moi

La ville est métallique et c'est la seule étoile
     Noyée dans tes yeux bleus
Quand les tramways roulaient jaillissaient des feux pâles
     Sur des oiseaux galeux

Et tout ce qui tremblait dans les yeux de mes songes
     Qu'un seul homme buvait
Sous les feux de gaz roux comme la fausse oronge
     O vêtue ton bras se lovait

Vois l'histrion tire la langue aux attentives
     Un fantôme s'est suicidé
L'apôtre au figuier pend et lentement salive
     Jouons donc cet amour aux dés

Des cloches aux sons clairs annonçaient ta naissance
                  Vois
Les chemins sont fleuris et les palmes s'avancent
                 Vers toi

                         (Un Soir, OP, p. 126)

8. CAPITAL EXECUTION

Zone (Zone): Finished in September or October, 1912, according to M. Décaudin, and published for the first time
in the Soirées *de Paris* (December, 1912). Let us note
that the publication of Cendrars's *Easter* was scheduled
for October 26, in the magazine *Les Hommes nouveaux*.

Finally you are tired of this ancient world

Shepherdess O Eiffel tower the flock of bridges is bleat-
                           ing this morning

You are tired of living in Greek and Roman antiquity

Here even the automobiles seem to be ancient
Only religion has remained totally new religion
Has remained simple like the hangars of the airfield

Alone in Europe you are not ancient O Christian faith
The most modern European is you Pope Pius X
And you whom the windows are watching shame is holding
                                        you back
From entering a church for confession this morning
You are reading prospectuses catalogues posters
                                which sing aloud
That is poetry this morning and as for prose there
                                are newspapers
There are 25 cent publications full of detective stories
Portraits of great men and a thousand various titles

This morning I saw a pretty street whose name I
                                have forgotten
New and clean it was the sun's bugle
Executive workers and the beautiful stenographers
From Monday morning to Saturday night go by there
                                four times a day
In the morning three times the siren wails there
An angry bell barks there towards noon
The inscriptions on the billboards and the walls
The plaques and notices cry out like parrots
I love the grace of this industrial street
Located in Paris between the rue Aumon-Thiéville
                                and the Avenue des Ternes

Here is the young street and you are still nothing but
                                a little child
Your mother dresses you only in blue and white
You are very pious and with your oldest friend René Dalize
You love nothing so much as the pomp of the church
It is nine o'clock the gas is down and blue you sneak out
                                of the dormitory
You pray all night in the school chapel
While eternal and adorable an amethyst depth
Turns forever the blazing glory of Christ
It is the beautiful lily that we all cultivate
It is the red-headed torch that the wind does not
                                blow out
It is the pale and vermilion son of the dolorous mother
It is the tree always thick with all the prayers

It is the double gallows of honor and eternity
It is the six-pronged star
It is God who dies on Friday and resuscitates on Sunday
It is Christ who soars to the sky better than the aviators
He holds the world's altitude record
Christ pupil of the eye
Twentieth pupil of the centuries he knows how to go
                              about it
And turned into a bird this century like Jesus soars
                              into the air
The devils in the abysses raise their heads to look at him
They say he is imitating Simon Magus in Judea
They shout that if he knows how to fly he should be called
                              a flier-thief
Angels hover around the pretty aerialist
Icarus Enoch Elijah Apollonius of Tyana
Float around the first airplane
Sometimes they move aside to make way for those who are
                              carried by the Holy Eucharist
Those priests who rise eternally elevating the Host
The airplane lands at last without folding its wings
The sky fills up then with millions of swallows
Swiftly come the crows the falcons the owls
From Africa arrive ibises flamingoes marabous
The Roc bird celebrated by story tellers and poets
Glides holding in his claws Adam's skull the first head
The eagle sweeps down from the horizon with a great cry
And from America comes the tiny humming-bird
From China have come the long and supple pihis
Which have only one wing and fly in couples
Then here is the dove immaculate spirit
Escorted by the lyre bird and the ocellated peacock
The phoenix pyre which recreates itself
For an instant veils everything with his burning ashes
The syrens leaving their perilous straights
Arrive all three singing beautifully
And all of them eagle phoenix and pihis from China
Fraternize with the flying machine

Now you are walking in Paris all alone in the crowd
Herds of bellowing buses roll by near you
The anguish of love clutches at your throat
As though you could never be loved again
If you lived in olden times you would enter a monastery
You are ashamed when you catch yourself saying a prayer
You are mocking yourself and like the fire of Hell your
                              laughter is crackling

The sparks of your laughter cast a glow upon the depth
                              of your life
It is a picture hanging in a gloomy museum
And sometimes you come to look at it closely

Today you are walking through Paris the women are
                              covered with blood
It was and I should prefer not to remember it was during
                              the decline of beauty

Surrounded by ardent flames Notre-Dame has looked at me
                              at Chartres
The blood of your Sacred Heart has flooded me in Montmartre
I am sick of hearing the blessed words
The love from which I suffer is a shameful sickness
And the image which posses you makes you live in insomnia
                              and anguish
It is always near you this passing image

Now you are by the shore of the Mediterranean
Under the lemon trees which flower all year
With your friends you are taking boat rides
One is a Nissard there is a Mentonasque and two
                              Turbiasques
We look with fear at the octopi of the deep
And among the algae swim the fish images of the Savior

You are in the garden of an inn on the outskirts
                              of Prague
You feel very happy a rose is on the table
And you are watching instead of writing your story
                              in prose
The rose beetle which is sleeping in the heart of the rose

Frightened you see yourself outlined in the agates
                              of St Vitus
You were sad enough to die on the day you saw yourself
                              there
You look like Lazarus maddened by daylight
The hands of the clock of the Jewish quarter
                              move backwards
And you are also slowly going backwards in your life
Climbing up to the Hradchin and listening at night
To the singing of Czech songs in the taverns

Here you are in Marseilles among the watermelons

Here you are in Coblenz at the Hotel of the Giant

Here you are in Rome seated under a Japanese medlar tree

Here you are in Amsterdam with a girl whom you find
                              beautiful and who is ugly
She is to marry a student from Leyden
They rent rooms there in Latin Cubicula locanda
I remember it I spent three days there and as many
                              at Gouda

You are in Paris before the examining magistrate
Like a criminal you are placed under arrest

You have taken painful and joyful trips
Before noticing the falsehood and the age
You have suffered from love at twenty and at thirty
I have lived like a crazyman and I have wasted my time
You no longer dare to look at your hands and at every
                              moment I would like to sob
About you about the one I love about everything which
                              has frightened you

You look at these poor emigrants with eyes full of tears
They believe in God they pray the women nurse
                              their children
Their odor fills the halls of the Gare St Lazare
They have faith in their star like the Magi
They hope to earn some money in Argentina
And to come back to their country having made
                              their fortune
A family carries a red quilt as you carry your heart
This quilt and our dreams are just as unreal
Some of these emigrants stay here and find lodging
In the slums of the rue des Rosiers or the rue
                              des Ecouffes
I have often seen them at night they take the air
                              in the street
And seldom move about like pieces in a chess game
There are mostly Jews their wives wear wigs
They remain seated bloodless in the rear of the shops

You are standing at the counter of a seamy bar
You take a two-cent cup of coffee among the poor

At night you are in a big restaurant

These women are not bad yet they have worries
All of them even the ugliest one have made their
                              lovers suffer
She is the daughter of a policeman from Jersey

Her hands which I had not seen are hard and chapped

I have immense pity for the scars on her belly

Now I humble my mouth by offering it to a poor girl
                              with a horrible laugh
You are alone the morning is coming
The milkmen rattle their cans in the streets

The night is leaving like a beautiful half-caste
It is the false Ferdine or the attentive Lea

And you are drinking this alcohol which burns like
                              your life
Your life which you are drinking like an *eau-de-vie*

You are walking towards Auteuil you want to go home
                              on foot
In order to sleep among your fetishes from Oceania
                              and Guinea
They are Christs of another form and another faith
They are the inferior Christs of obscure hopes

Farewell Farewell

Decapitated sun

                              (*Zone*, PW, pp. 39-44)

A la fin tu es las de ce monde ancien

Bergère ô tour Eiffel le troupeau des ponts bêle ce matin

Tu en as assez de vivre dans l'antiquité grecque
                              et romaine

Ici même les automobiles ont l'air d'être anciennes
La religion seule est restée toute neuve la religion
Est restée simple comme les hangars de Port-Aviation

Seul en Europe tu n'es pas antique ô Christianisme
L'Européen le plus moderne c'est vous Pape Pie X
Et toi que les fenêtres observent la honte te retient
D'entrer dans une église et de t'y confesser ce matin
Tu lis les prospectus les catalogues les affiches
                              qui chantent tout haut
Voilà la poésie ce matin et pour la prose il y a
                              les journaux
Il y a les livraisons à 25 centimes pleines
                              d'aventures policières
Portraits des grands hommes et mille titres divers

J'ai vu ce matin une jolie rue dont j'ai oublié le nom
Neuve et propre du soleil elle était le clairon

Les directeurs les ouvriers et les belles sténo-dactylo-
                          graphes
Du lundi matin au samedi soir quatre fois par jour
                    y passent
Le matin par trois fois la sirène y gémit
Une cloche rageuse y aboie vers midi
Les inscriptions des enseignes et des murailles
Les plaques les avis à la façon des perroquets criaillent
J'aime la grâce de cette rue industrielle
Située à Paris entre la rue Aumont-Thiéville et
                          l'avenue des Ternes

Voilà la jeune rue et tu n'es encore qu'un petit enfant
Ta mère ne t'habille que de bleu et de blanc
Tu es très pieux et avec le plus ancien de tes camarades
                    René Dalize
Vous n'aimez rien tant que les pompes de l'Église
Il est neuf heures le gaz est baissé tout bleu vous
                          sortez du dortoir en cachette
Vous priez toute la nuit dans la chapelle du collège
Tandis qu'éternelle et adorable profondeur améthyste
Tourne à jamais la flamboyante gloire du Christ
C'est le beau lys que tous nous cultivons
C'est la torche aux cheveux roux que n'éteint pas le vent
C'est le fils pâle et vermeil de la douloureuse mère
C'est l'arbre toujours touffu de toutes les prières
C'est la double potence de l'honneur et de l'éternité
C'est l'étoile à six branches
C'est Dieu qui meurt le vendredi et ressuscite le dimanche
C'est le Christ qui monte au ciel mieux que les aviateurs
Il détient le record du monde pour la hauteur

Pupille Christ de l'œil
Vingtième pupille des siècles il sait y faire
Et changé en oiseau ce siècle comme Jésus monte dans l'air
Les diables dans les abîmes lèvent la tête pour le regarder
Ils disent qu'il imite Simon Mage en Judée
Ils crient s'il sait voler qu'on l'appelle voleur
Les anges voltigent autour du joli voltigeur
Icare Énoch Élie Apollonius de Thyane
Flottent autour du premier aéroplane
Ils s'écartent parfois pour laisser passer ceux que trans-
                          porte la Sainte-Eucharistie
Ces prêtres qui montent éternellement élevant l'hostie
L'avion se pose enfin sans refermer les ailes
Le ciel s'emplit alors de millions d'hirondelles
A tire-d'aile viennent les corbeaux les faucons les hiboux

D'Afrique arrivent les ibis les flamants les marabouts
L'oiseau Roc célébré par les conteurs et les poètes
Plane tenant dans les serres le crâne d'Adam la
                          première tête
L'aigle fond de l'horizon en poussant un grand cri
Et d'Amérique vient le petit colibri
De Chine sont venus les pihis longs et souples
Qui n'ont qu'une seule aile et qui volent par couples
Puis voici la colombe esprit immaculé
Qu'escortent l'oiseau-lyre et le paon ocellé
Le phénix ce bûcher qui soi-même s'engendre
Un instant voile tout de son ardente cendre
Les sirènes laissant les périlleux détroits
Arrivent en chantant bellement toutes trois
Et tous aigle phénix et pihis de la Chine
Fraternisent avec la volante machine

Maintenant tu marches dans Paris tout seul parmi la foule
Des troupeaux d'autobus mugissants près de toi roulent
L'angoisse de l'amour te serre le gosier
Comme si tu ne devais jamais plus être aimé
Si tu vivais dans l'ancien temps tu entrerais dans
                          un monastère
Vous avez honte quand vous vous surprenez à dire
                          une prière
Tu te moques de toi et comme le feu de l'Enfer ton
                          rire pétille
Les étincelles de ton rire dorent le fond de ta vie
C'est un tableau pendu dans un sombre musée
Et quelquefois tu vas le regarder de près

Aujourd'hui tu marches dans Paris les femmes
                          sont ensanglantées
C'était et je voudrais ne pas m'en souvenir c'était au
                          déclin de la beauté
Entourée de flammes ferventes Notre-Dame m'a
                          regardé à Chartres
Le sang de votre Sacré-Coeur m'a inondé à Montmartre
Je suis malade d'ouïr les paroles bienheureuses
L'amour dont je souffre est une maladie honteuse
Et l'image qui te possède te fait survivre dans l'insomnie
                          et dans l'angoisse
C'est toujours près de toi cette image qui passe

Maintenant tu es au bord de la Méditerranée
Sous les citronniers qui sont en fleur toute l'année
Avec tes amis tu te promènes en barque

L'un est Nissard il y a un Mentonasque et deux Turbiasques
Nous regardons avec effroi les poulpes des profondeurs
Et parmi les algues nagent les poissons images du Sauveur

Tu es dans le jardin d'une auberge aux environs de Prague
Tu te sens tout heureux une rose est sur la table
Et tu observes au lieu d'écrire ton conte en prose
La cétoine qui dort dans le coeur de la rose

Épouvanté tu te vois dessiné dans les agates de Saint-Vit
Tu étais triste à mourir le jour où tu t'y vis
Tu ressembles au Lazare affolé par le jour
Les aiguilles de l'horloge du quartier juif
                    vont à rebours
Et tu recules aussi dans ta vie lentement
En montant au Hradchin et le soir en écoutant
Dans les tavernes chanter des chansons tchèques

Te voici à Marseille au milieu des pastèques

Te voilà à Coblence à l'hôtel du Géant

Te voici à Rome assis sous un néflier du Japon

Te voici à Amsterdam avec une jeune fille que tu trouves
                    belle et qui est laide
Elle doit se marier avec un étudiant de Leyde
On y loue des chambres en latin Cubicula locanda
Je m'en souviens j'y ai passé trois jours et autant
                    à Gouda

Tu es à Paris chez le juge d'instruction
Comme un criminel on te met en état d'arrestation

Tu as fait de douloureux et de joyeux voyages
Avant de t'apercevoir du mensonge et de l'âge
Tu as souffert de l'amour à vingt et à trente ans
J'ai vécu comme un fou et j'ai perdu mon temps
Tu n'oses plus regarder tes mains et à tous moments
                    je voudrais sangloter
Sur toi sur celle que j'aime sur tout ce qui
                    t'a époutvanté

Tu regardes les yeux pleins de larmes ces pauvres
                    émigrants
Ils croient en Dieu ils prient les femmes allaitent
                    des enfants
Ils emplissent de leur odeur le hall de la gare
                    Saint-Lazare
Ils ont foi dans leur étoile comme les rois-mages

Ils espèrent gagner de l'argent dans l'Argentine
Et revenir dans leur pays après avoir fait fortune
Une famille transporte un édredon rouge comme vous trans-
                           portez votre coeur
Cet édredon et nos rêves sont aussi irréels
Quelques-uns de ces émigrants restent ici et se logent
Rue des Rosiers ou rue des Écouffes dans les bouges
Je les ai vus souvent le soir ils prennent l'air
                           dans la rue
Et se déplacent rarement comme les pièces aux échecs
Il y a surtout des Juifs leurs femmes portent perruque
Elles restent assises exsangues au fond des boutiques

Tu es debout devant le zinc d'un bar crapuleux
Tu prends un café à deux sous parmi les malheureux

Tu es la nuit dans un grand restaurant

Ces femmes ne sont pas méchantes elles ont des
                           soucis cependant
Toutes même la plus laide a fait souffrir son amant
Elle est la fille d'un sergent de ville de Jersey

Ses mains que je n'avais pas vues sont dures et gercées

J'ai une pitié immense pour les coutures de son ventre

J'humilie maintenant à une pauvre fille au rire
                           horrible ma bouche
Tu es seul le matin va venir
Les laitiers font tinter leurs bidons dans les rues

La nuit s'éloigne ainsi qu'une belle métive
C'est Ferdine la fausse ou Léa l'attentive

Et tu bois cet alcool brûlant comme ta vie
Ta vie que tu bois comme une eau-de-vie

Tu marches vers Auteuil tu veux aller chez toi à pied
Dormir parmi tes fétiches d'Océanie et de Guinée
Ils sont des Christ d'une autre forme et d'une
                           autre croyance
Ce sont les Christ inférieurs des obscures espérances

Adieu Adieu

Soleil cou coupé

                           (*Zone*, OP, pp. 39-44)

9. ON THE RUINS OF CHRISTIANISM, THE RELIGION OF HONOR

The Seated Woman (La Femme assise): Before the war of 1914,
Apollinaire thought of writing a novel about the Mormons.
He finished it in 1917-18, leaving two similar manu-
scripts. This excerpt seems to date from 1918.

...Anatole de Saintariste considered his time if not
scornfully at least with an astonishment mingled with a
horror of severity.

His thoughts and his inclination led him to imagine a
religion of honor.

Saintariste lived on rue Delambre, and, one evening,
greeting Ovide de Pont-Euxin, he told him immediately:
"See in me nothing but a sort of monk whose life, or rather what remains of it, will be devoted to the accomplish-
ment of the mission which I have given to myself.

"For me, it is a question of founding a religion without
dogmas and without priests in which the important thing
will be the moral and physical education of children.   You
will tell me that it is an idea that could only come to a
soldier and I admit it.   I was a soldier and my soul has
remained that of a soldier. The renewal of religious fervor which one notices everywhere is misleading. All religions are near death and are becoming extremely vague.
Today, superstitions and religious beliefs are contiguous
to such an extent that one would have to be very clever
indeed to be able to delineate the exact limit of one or
the other, and this happens in the very bosom of the same
religion.

"Today one can see what could only be seen in the Roman
Empire and at the end of paganism: the faithful who practice a religion, uphold it, defend it, and honor it without believing in it.   People have become aware of this at
last.   The truism which says that the people need a religion is true to the letter, but the people, without being
happier for it, now examine beliefs.   And today, faith
without calculation is rare; it will become more so, or
else it will apply only to extremely vague beliefs, or it
will again suddenly fall into the worst and the most pre-
posterous superstitions.   Belgian Antoinism, Rasputinism,
and all the mystical follies of the Russians, without speaking of the thousand absurdities which are born daily in
the five parts of the world, are some of the examples of
the stupidities to which the popular soul can give birth
tomorrow in a country even as well policed as France. Don't

forget Deacon Pâris, and let us not speak of anything contemporary. A religion of honor would avoid such errors
for an enlightened humanity. It allows, above all, elim-
ination of the fables of expiation and reward, which are
the most dangerous inventions of the founders of religion.
Honor has always been a type of rare superiority given to
certain men. Today they meet in war, and hardly anywhere
else. There is much to say on this subject, but one can
argue that, practically speaking, the feeling of honor has
disappeared from the earth, except for certain admirable
cases and those in which, without diminishing their value,
honor is born of necessity, such as war.

"Religions promised rewards in the next world. Socio-
logists promise to the individual happiness in this world.
All this must be eliminated, and men must find happiness
from now on only in themselves, through the satisfaction
of an accomplished duty and a preserved honor."

> (*The Seated Woman,* Gallimard, 1948, pp. 147ff;
> OC, pp. 435-36)

...Anatole de Saintariste regardait son temps, sinon
avec mépris, du moins avec un étonnement mêlé d'horreur de
sévérité.

Ses réflexions et son penchant l'amenèrent à imaginer une
religion d'honneur.

Saintariste habitait rue Delambre et un soir accueillant
Ovide de Pont-Euxin lui dit aussitôt: "Ne voyez en moi
qu'une sorte de moine, dont la vie, ou plutôt ce qui m'en
reste, sera consacré à l'accomplissement de la mission que
je me suis donnée.

"Il s'agit pour moi de fonder une religion sans dogmes
et sans prêtres où l'éducation morale et physique des enfants sera la grande affaire. Vous me direz que c'est une
idée qui ne pouvait venir qu'à un soldat et je vous l'ac-
corde. J'ai été soldat et mon âme est restée celle d'un
soldat. Le renouveau de l'idée religieuse que l'on constate partout est trompeur. Toutes les religions sont près
de mourir et deviennent d'un vague extrême. Superstitions
et croyances religieuses confinent aujourd'hui à un tel
point que bien malin qui voudrait marquer la limite exacte
des unes et des autres et au sein même d'une seule religion.

"On voit aujourd'hui ce qui ne s'était vu que dans l'Empire romain et à la fin du paganisme: des fidèles qui
observent une religion, la soutiennent, la défendent et
l'honorent sans y croire. On s'en est rendu compte désor-

mais; le lieu commun qui dit que le peuple a besoin d'une
religion est vrai à la lettre, mais le peuple, sans être
plus heureux pour cela, examine maintenant les croyances.
Et la foi sans calcul est rare aujourd'hui, elle le de-
viendra de plus en plus, ou bien ne s'appliquera qu'à des
croyances extrêmement vagues, ou encore tombera soudain
dans les pires et les plus saugrenues des superstitions.
L'antoinisme belge, le raspoutinisme et toutes les folies
mystiques des Russes, sans parler des milles absurdités qui
naissent quotidiennement dans les cinq parties du monde,
sont des exemples des imbécillités que l'âme populaire peut
enfanter demain dans un pays même aussi policé que la
France. N'oubliez pas le diacre Pâris pour ne parler de
rien qui soit contemporain. La religion de l'honneur évi-
terait à l'humanité avertie des écarts semblables. Elle
permet de supprimer avant tout les fables de l'expiation
et de la récompense qui sont les inventions les plus dangereuses qu'aient faites les fondateurs de religion. L'honneur a toujours été une sorte de rare supériorité dévolue
à certains hommes. Ils se rencontrent aujourd'hui à la
guerre et guère ailleurs. Il y aurait beaucoup à dire à ce
sujet, mais on peut soutenir que pratiquement parlant, le
sentiment de l'honneur a disparu de la terre sauf certains
cas admirables et ceux où sans les dimminuer il vient de ˚
la nécessité, ainsi à la guerre.

"Les religions promettaient des récompenses dans l'autre
monde, les sociologues promettent aux individus le bonheur
de ce monde; il faut supprimer tout cela et que les hommes
ne trouvent désormais le bonheur qu'en eux-mêmes par la
satisfaction du devoir accompli et de l'honneur sauve-
gardé."

(*La Femme Assise,* Gallimard, 1948, pp. 147sq.;
OC, pp. 435-36)

10. THE TWILIGHT OF THE GODS

Color of Time (Couleur du Temps): Written in 1918, this
drama was in rehearsal when Apollinaire died; it was per-
formed on November 24, 1918, and published in the *Nouvelle
Revue Française* in November, 1920).

...I see them arriving they are the Mavise gods
The gods yes all the gods of our humanity
Who are gathering here and indeed it is without a doubt
The first time that it is happening to them
The gods of wood of stone and of gold the subtle gods

And those of thought come toward the sun
The universe in their shadow oscillates with terror
And even the atmosphere is completely troubled
Bel ploughs the immensity with his twelve horns
All the temples have opened and all the gods
Have come from everywhere to speak to the sun
All are good even those who love victims
They have always wanted peace for their faithful
Most of them love man and would like him to be good
They wish that death would never be given
They wish that only for them offerings be sacrificed
Sacred pawns of peace between man and life
The most bloody the most cruel love peace
And that is why they all come to consult
This great sun who vivifies us all
See these gods they are an unfurled sea
It is a great fire which advances and bellows
Here are the old genii bulls with a human forehead
Whose beard is flowing and is dressed in the miter
All these monstrous gods darken the azure
The gods of Babylon and all the gods of Assur
Here is Melquarth the boatman and the moloch
The starved one who always nourishes his ardent belly
Baal with the many names adored on the coasts
This whirling Belzebuth God of the flies
And of battlefields listen listen
Tanit comes crying and Lilith is lamenting
And on a throne made of layered flames
Of frightened angels and of celestial flames
Terrible and magnificent surrounded by golden wings
By luminous circles with a moving light
Yahweh the jealous whose name is terrifying
Arrives fulgurating infinite adorable
Here are gods more gods more gods
All the ancient gods coming from the pyramids
Sphinxes gods of Egypt with animal heads
Osiris and the gods of Greece
The muses the three sisters Hermes the Dioscures
Jupiter Apollo and all the gods of Virgil
And the tragic cross from which the blood is flowing
Through the wounded forehead through the five
                                            divine wounds
Dominates the sun who adores it while trembling
Here are the manitos the American gods
The spirits of the snow and their Ganic flies

The Gallic Teutates the Nordic Walkyries
The Indian temples have also emptied
All the assembled gods weep to see men
Killing each other under the sun who is also weeping
Sun O life O life
Appease the angers
Console the regrets
Have mercy on men
Have mercy on gods
The gods who are going to die
If humanity dies...

> (*Color of Time*, Act III, Scene I,
> PW, pp. 949-50)

...Je les vois arriver ce sont les dieux Mavise
Les dieux oui tous les dieux de notre humanité
Qui s'assemblent ici et c'est sans aucun doute
Bien la première fois que cela leur arrive
Les dieux de bois de pierre et d'or les dieux subtils
Et ceux de la pensée viennent vers le soleil
L'univers sous leur ombre oscille de terreur
Et l'atmosphère même en est toute troublée
Bel fend l'immensité avec ses douze cornes
Tous les temples se sont ouverts et tous les dieux
Sont venus de partout pour parler au soleil
Tous sont bons même ceux qui aiment les victimes
Ils ont toujours voulu la paix de leurs croyants
La plupart aiment l'homme et voudraient qu'il soit bon
Ils voudraient que jamais on ne donnât la mort
Ils veulent qu'à eux seuls s'immolent les hosties
Gages sacrés de paix entre l'homme et la vie
Les plus sanglants les plus cruels aiment la paix
Et c'est pourquoi ils viennent tous se concerter
Avec ce grand soleil qui nous vivifie tous
Voyez ces dieux ce sont une mer déchaînée
C'est un grand incendie qui s'avance et qui gronde
Voici les vieux génies taureaux au front humain
Dont la barbe ruisselle et coiffée de la mitre
Tous ces dieux monstrueux obscurcissent l'azur
Les dieux de Babylone et tous les dieux d'Assur
Voici Melquarth le nautonier et le moloch
L'afflamé qui toujours nourrit son ventre ardent
Baal au nom multiple adoré sur les côtes
Ce tourbillonnement Belzébuth Dieu des mouches
Et des champs de bataille écoutez écountez

Tanit vient en criant et Lilith se lamente
Et sur un trône fait de flammes étagées
D'anges épouvantés et de flammes célestes
Terrible et magnifique entouré d'ailes d'or
De cercles lumineux à la lueur mouvante
Jéhovah le jaloux dont le nom épouvante
Arrive fulgurant infini adorable
Voici des dieux toujours des dieux toujours des dieux
Tous les antiques dieux venus des pyramides
Les sphinx les dieux d'Égypte aux têtes d'animaux
Les nomes Osiris et les dieux de la Grèce
Les muses les trois sœurs Hermès les Dioscures
Jupiter Apollon tous les dieux de Virgile
Et la tragique croix d'où le sang coule à flots
Par le front écorché par les cinq plaies divines
Domine le soleil qui l'adore en tremblant
Voilà les manitous les dieux américains
Les esprits de la neige et leurs mouches ganiques
Les Teutatès gaulois les walkyries nordiques
Les temples indiens se sont aussi vidés
Tous les dieux assemblés pleurent de voir les hommes
S'entretuer sous le soleil qui pleure aussi
Soleil ô vie ô vie
Apaise les colères
Console les regrets
Prends en pitié les hommes
Prends en pitié les Dieux
Les Dieux qui vont mourir
Si l'humanité meurt...

                    (*Couleur du temps*, acte III, scène 1,
                                        OP, pp. 949-50)

Bibliographical Note

Before all, and precluding almost everything else, Marie-Jeanne Durry's course devoted to *Alcools*! The two chapters--chapters VII and VIII--of her first volume, entitled "Apollinaire and Religion," and "Of the Religious Feeling in Apollinaire and of a Few Poems of *Alcools*" (S.E.D.E.S., 1956), constitute the most complete and the richest study of Apollinaire's religion. However, we think that the order in which the poems of Cendrars and of Apollinaire are discussed should be inverted; in our opinion, it is the latter who is the more religious, for one feels in Apollinaire's work a revival of a faith that was real, whereas the poet of *Easter*, Cendrars, has never had anything but an inclination toward faith.

Among the studies that preceded Marie-Jeanne Durry's book, let us mention a thesis from the University of Paris (typewritten) by Justine Krug: "The Mythological References in the *Oeuvre* of Guillaume Apollinaire" ("Les Références à la mythologie dans l'oeuvre de Guillaume Apollinaire") (1951). A section of this work is dedicated to Judeo-Christian mythology, but the author sees in this only one mythology among others, and one less favored, in her opinion, than the Greek; she is not concerned, and this was not her aim, with the religious feelings of the poet of *Zone*.

On the other hand, Margaret Davies' 1948 university thesis, *The Irony of Guillaume Apollinaire (L'Ironie de Guillaume Apollinaire)*, considered only the antireligious and anticlerical aspect of his works, perhaps exaggerating it to the point of missing all positive traces of his childhood religion.

Jeanine Moulin, in her *Guillaume Apollinaire* (unpublished texts with an introduction), Droz, 1952, had foreseen the religious value of *Zone*, but she seems, in our opinion, to minimize the religious anxiety that can be felt in the rest of Apollinaire's oeuvre.

Subsequent to Marie-Jeanne Durry's work, several articles have treated the question of Apollinaire's religion, either directly or in passing. The article of Jean Bertrand-Barrère, "The Obscene and Tender Apollinaire" ("Apollinaire obscène et tendre") in the *Revue des Sciences Humaines,* 1956--the issue dedicated to Guillaume Apollinaire--is always fresh, judicious, full of irony. But Barrère does not take the poet seriously enough and, for instance, throws a doubt on the religious value of the versets of *Zone* ("mys-

tical or pretending to be so...") and denies all sense of
sin in the poet of *The Gipsy*.

There is not much to say about a German article by Fritz
Werf: "Remarks on the theme of Apollinaire and religion"
("Amerkungen zu dem Thema Apollinaire und die Religion,")
published in *Antarès*, in June, 1958. A few texts are presented; the author wonders about the poet's contradictions
but fails to explain them.

A good article on "Apollinaire and the Sacred" ("Apollinaire et le sacré") in *Critique* (August-September, 1958),
by Jean Roudaut, is right, in our opinion, in depicting
Apollinaire as "anxious about the sacred," but sees in him
no religious elements. It was during the war that Apollinaire, according to Roudaut, found the sacred element
par excellence.

A remarkable article by S.I. Lockerbie: "*Alcools* and
Symbolism" ("*Alcools* et le symbolisme") in the *Revue des
Lettres modernes* (1963), contributes by ascribing more so-
lidity to Apollinaire's work than is usually done. Lockerbie has the merit of having discovered a theme, like
Ariadne's thread, running through the large poems of *Alcools*: the quest for the absolute. He has no difficulty
in showing that the poems dealing with the end of a love
are filled with quasimetaphysical yearning and are also
poems dealing with the end of the world. His study brings
out the religious significance (though Lockerbie does not
use this word) of *The Song of the Poorly Loved*, of *The
Traveller*, of *Zone*, in the sense that these poems (and
others) are a tragic questioning on the meaning of existence. He has been able to compare T. S. Elliot's *Waste
Land* to these poems from *Alcools* without exaggeration, because both poets are engaged in a same spiritual adven-
ture. However, Lockerbie should have discerned that this
absolute is not a vague infinite but a faith in the Christian God of Apollinaire's youth, as the typical quotations
which he gives clearly demonstrate.

André Fonteyne has recently published a work on *Apollinaire the Prose Writer: The Heresiarch and Co.* (*Apollinaire prosateur: l'Hérésiarque et Cie*, Nizet, 1964). His
study, which is serious and methodical as well as subtle
and sensitive, finds a religious theme in each page and
puts back in a place of honor "the forgotten side of Apollinaire's religiosity." Fonteyne has shown that the attacks against Christianism often express the storyteller's
personal bitterness, and that the characters are "the
mouthpieces...of Apollinaire's own grievances"--and we

entirely agree with him. Our study of the poems confirms the conclusions reached by Fonteyne after his analysis of the stories of *The Heresiarch and Co.*

One must add to this list the names of two of the most enlightened critics of Apollinaire's oeuvre who, without making Apollinaire's religion the object of one of their studies, knew how to recognize its importance even if they don't develop this theme.

Margaret Davies, in her *Apollinaire* (Oliver & Boyd, 1964), after having insisted in her first chapters on the influence of Apollinaire's religious education, discusses in several places the preoccupations, scruples, and renewal of faith of the poet of *Alcools.*

Michel Décaudin, the most prolific, the most serious, perhaps the most cautious of Apollinaire's commentators, has given to the poet's genius its true dimensions, and therefore the religious dimension. In his thesis on the *Crisis of Symbolist Values, Twenty Years of French Poetry, 1895-1914 (Crise des valeurs symbolistes, Vingt ans de poésie française, 1895-1914,* Privat, 1960), he has brought together the great names of Claudel, Milosz, Saint-John Perse, Jules Romains with that of Apollinaire, showing a "mystical movement...a spiritual exercise, a quest for God in the desperate cry of *Zone* or in that of *Easter."* The entire book is full of suggestive remarks on all the subjects concerning Apollinaire and, thus, that of religion. Let us recall the *Dossier d'Alcools* (Droz & Minard, 1960), and the issues of the *Revue des Lettres Modernes* dedicated to Guillaume Apollinaire, every year since 1962 (Minard).

Finally, André Rouveyre, especially in *Love and Poetry of Apollinaire (Amour et poésie d'Apollinaire,* Paris, Ed. du Seuil, 1955), has noted Apollinaire's "intimate impregnation" with things religious, but he has unduly exaggerated it.

We should like to refer the reader to our own work *Apollinaire and the Bible (Apollinaire et la Bible,* Minard, 1966), which provides a more thorough and more detailed study of Apollinaire's religion, from a more precise point of departure.

Index

Adam, 17,22,93
Al-David, 34,36,37
Alexander VI Borgia, 48
Angélique (in *The Putrescent Magician*), 25
Angelica or Angélique. See Kostrowitzky, Angélique de
Apollinaire, Guillaume: chronology, vi-xi; youth, 5-10,12,13,15-18; loss of faith, 20-25,27-29,31-35, 37,39,40,42-45,47-50; longings, regrets and confidences, 51,53,57-59, 61; Santé episode, 62-65; *Zone*, 66-86; post *Zone* period, 87-104; *Alcools*, xi,4,5,14,51, 55,56,62,65,85,88,96, 99,104,110,117,136,153, 154,155; *Anecdotes (Anecdotiques)*, 94; *The Bestiary or Cortege of Orpheus (Le Bestiaire ou cortège d'Orphée)*, x,57-59,61,81; *The Betrothal (Les Fiançailles)*, x,55,56, 59,60,69,85; *The Blue Eye (L'Oeil bleu)*, 6; *The Brasier (Le Brasier)*, x,51, 55,110; *The Breasts of Tiresias (Les Mamelles de Tirésias)*, xii; *Calligrammes,* xii,88,98,99; *The Clowns of Elvira (Les clowns d'Elvire)*, xi; *Color of Time (Couleur du Temps)*, xii, 99, 101,102,149; *The Dancer (La Danseuse)*, 42,43; *Death of Pan (Mort de Pan)*, ix,17,

22,85; *The Disappearance of Honoré Subrac (La Disaparition d' Honoré Subrac)*, 34; *The Dome of Cologne (Le Dôme de Cologne)*, 20,30, 45,49,59,79,85,98,127; *The Door (La Porte)*, 52; *Eau-de-vie*, xi; *The Elegy of the Traveller with Wounded Feet (L'élégie du voyageur aux pieds blessés)*, 26; *The End of Babylon (La Fin de Babylone)*, 47,48; *Giovanni Moroni*, 10-12, 45,49; *The Gipsy (La Tzigane)*, 53,85,154; *The Heresiarch and Co. (L'Hérésiarque et Cie.)*, ix,x,3,4,10,12,22,34,37, 41,42,46,48-51,61,62,68, 69,73,87,100,102,130, 154,155; *The Hermit (L'Ermite)*, 27,28,49,52; *The Hills (Les Collines)*, 62,83,97,98; *Hunting Horn (Cors de chasse)*, 66; *Infallibility (L'Infaillibilité)*, 37-39, 130; *The Latin Jew (Le Juif latin)*, 38,43,45, 46; *The Lectern (Le Lutrin)*, 39; *Letters to Madeleine (Lettres à Madeleine)*, 93,101; *Marie*, 66; *The Masters of Love (Les Maîtres de l'amour)*, 3; *The Mirabeau Bridge (Le Pont Mirabeau)*, 3,66; *Of a*

156